Women's Ways, Women's Plays

*The story of
Corby Women's Theatre Group*

Paula Boulton

Copyright © Paula Boulton
Photo Credits
Kate Dyer: Vagina Monologues, Heritage. Author photo
Lola Dziarkowska: WOS, About Her, OBOS
For further photo credits contact the author

Typeset by Craig Barber
Cover design Kate Anderson

First published in the UK in 2023
by Lunarlink Publishing Collective
43 Epsom Walk, Corby, Northants
NN18 9JJ

Printed by Ingram Spark

A catalogue number for this book is available from the British Library

ISBN 978-1-906482-09-1

**Lunarlink Publishing
Collective**

In memory of
Josie Cassidy,
Bridie Norton
and
Joy Elizabeth Surgey

Also by Paula Boulton

Women of Steel: A Living History of Corby
First edition: Corby Zone 2008
Second edition: Completely Novel 2018

Impressions of an English Woodland
First edition: Completely Novel 2019
Second edition: Lunarlink Publishing Collective 2020
Illustrated edition: Lunarlink Publishing Collective 2020

Inspiring Kingswood
Lunarlink Publishing Collective 2020

Steel Kids: Shouting for 20 years
Lunarlink Publishing Collective 2022

Issue-based plays for young people
Lunarlink Publishing Collective 2022

Lunarlink Publishing
Collective

Intro:

During COVID lockdown, my project *Shouting for 20 years* documented and archived the 20-year history of my youth theatre group Shout! Theatre. It involved holding a reunion, producing a film, launching a website, creating working scripts for schools and publishing an anthology of all the plays we had created over the years. That book - *Steel Kids* - also told the story of the group.

Since the Corby Women's Theatre Group emerged at about the same time, I thought that its 20-year herstory deserved the same recognition. So I applied for funding to do a similar project to *Shouting for 20 years*, and got it. The *Corby Women, Then and Now* project has two parts; this book, which tells the story of the theatre group and archives the plays we put on over 20 years, and a new play for performance at the Core Theatre in October 2023.

I hope that the book gives an insight into and an understanding of the lives of the women of Corby. Their tales will resonate with working-class women everywhere, but especially those in post-industrial areas. And if you have picked up this book in search of plays by women, for women, you are in for a rare treat. Each one is totally unique in structure and you have my express permission to adapt them to suit your group, place and time.

With characters ranging from cleaners to care workers, suffragettes to steel workers – I am sure you will find plenty of realistic characters to get your teeth into, as actors or readers.

This book may be a "how to" manual for you or a "how was it?" documentary history. Whether it is methodology or memento, I hope you enjoy *Women's Ways, Women's Plays*.

Paula Boulton
8th March 2023

CONTENTS

The Story of
Corby Women's Theatre Group

In 1986 a group of women in Corby started meeting to discuss the problems we as women were facing at the time. Thatcher's Britain was taking a severe toll on women, and from our informal chats we began to realise that since these things were happening to women and not men, it must be to do with us being women. We didn't have words like sex-class, or patriarchy, or even sexism. We didn't know that our informal sharing was being mirrored in other towns and cities and would be called consciousness-raising. Women everywhere were waking up and standing up.

The motto of our town is Deeds not Words. So we decided we needed somewhere where women could gather "to decide for themselves their needs, social, cultural, emotional, physical and educational, and through mutual self- help and empowerment take steps to meet those needs". That was the stated aim of the Women's Centre which we eventually founded. How did it happen?

I was teaching study skills for the Corby Unemployed Activities Centre (C.U.A.C.) in the Welfare Rights building, which was a small hut on a rooftop carpark. One day after class, out of curiosity, I opened the door into the room adjoining the hall – a small 6ft by 20 ft office with a cloakroom and an outside door. It was unused. I persuaded the manager of the building to let us use it, and on Dec 14th 1986 a group of us from Corby Women for Peace went alternative carol-singing and ended up back at our new Women's Centre with a bottle of cider bought from the proceeds, and toasted our first home. We would have several others before we eventually closed the doors 24 years later.

Very quickly we realised how difficult things were for women and how many services we considered essential just didn't exist. This was DIY time. Before long we were running free pregnancy testing, dealing with cases of domestic violence (as it was called in those days), training with Rape Crisis in London, supporting women through their post-rape ordeals, attending employment tribunals and child custody cases, and building up a huge file of information and referral points. We ran self-help groups for everything from menopause to widowhood to prison visiting. We started a group for girls, introducing them to carpentry and broadening their horizons in general.

We also ran some adult education classes for women. My background was in the Performing Arts, so I set up Creative Dance classes and Drama classes. The sessions were fun and emboldening for the women. Initially I struggled to find suitable plays with decent parts and relevant stories, but eventually I found the Methuen Plays by Women series, which led to a hilarious term working on Sue Townsend's *Womberang,* a comedy set in a gynaecologist's waiting room.

The funding ran out – but the idea stayed. And so did the Tory government.

By 1994, becoming increasingly outraged by the impact of Tory policies, I decided that I had to change my focus and do all I could to bring about a change of government. A turning point came on May Day, when my dad suggested I use my existing skills in the Arts to raise awareness of the many injustices we were witnessing daily. Corby had struggled to rebuild itself after the destruction of the steel industry, and as a town we had huge social problems - many of which we were dealing with at the Women's Centre.

It so happened that Tony Benn was speaking at the local theatre that very evening. Coincidence or cosmic design, who knows: I went along for inspiration and heard his support act, Banner Theatre, a political theatre company which tours to a labour movement/trade union base with plays about the realities faced by working-class people. They had been a great support to Corby people during the steel strike, documenting the situation by writing *Steel.*

I had previously lived in Holland where I was part of a political theatre group, Beroerd. We made and toured plays about the current situation in Latin America. I loved the Banner performance, and speaking afterwards to Aidan Jolly, one of the band, I mentioned that I was interested in finding my way back into political theatre but in the UK. It so happened that Banner had just advertised for a new member to join them on their upcoming tour, *Sweatshop* – a play which had been partly researched in Corby. This was one of many "meant-to-be" moments in my life. I auditioned, got taken on, and toured with them for four years learning all the ins and outs of documentary political theatre along the way.

On my return to Corby, I started my own company *Shout! Youth Theatre,* and set about making plays telling the reality of young people's lives using the techniques I had learned during my time with Banner.

Having established myself as a playwright and theatre director in the town, I was approached by Kate Dyer from Corby Community Arts, who wanted to put on a performance of Eve Ensler's Vagina Monologues.

The original cast of Vagina Monologues at the ARC Theatre 2003

The idea of a Corby Women's Theatre Group came from the women who had taken part in that performance and the subsequent one the following year. They enjoyed the experience so much they wanted it to continue. So I approached the Worker's Educational Association, and sold them the idea of a course called "Creating a Community Drama". My intention was to create our own plays to tell our own stories.

We also wanted to establish a tradition of performing on International Women's Day. Though the women had enjoyed taking part in the *Vagina Monologues,* one of them remarked, "We're more than a vagina, why not focus on our whole body?"– so we set about creating our first play *"Our Bodies, Ourselves"* to be ready for March 8th 2005. The title is that of the well-known women's health "bible", and we were granted permission by the Boston Women's Health Collective, who created the original book, to use the title for our purposes.

"Our Bodies, Ourselves," gave me the opportunity to teach the group devising and acting skills and to show how a simple play could be put together. What we needed next was a project which would involve the community, and teach the women documentary theatre research techniques.

Banner productions were always based on true stories and incorporated the words of working-class people describing their own reality. A team of researchers would head off into the community to find people to interview. I remember when we were researching for *Criminal Justice* - a play which exposed the erosion of civil liberties by the 1994 Criminal Justice Act and highlighted the resistance by a wide range of groups, which were adversely affected by it. The research team interviewed around 80 people affected by the legislation, ranging from Anti-M11 link road campaigners, disabled activists and "new-age" travellers through to gypsies, squatters and "Footballers against the CJA".

We were deliberately assigned to groups we knew least about to avoid already having a filter in place. I headed off to interview gypsies, squatters, football supporters, road protesters and the lollipop lady from Wanstead.

Once the interview team reconvened, the battle to get our favourite stories included would begin. Recording people sharing their real-life experiences was very moving. I always became attached and found it hard to get excited by the interviews anyone else was enthusing about. But ultimately the playwright had to create a balanced piece out of a surplus of material, and so had the final say.

Once the skeleton was in place and we knew which stories were to be used - we began the long process of listening to the tapes and selecting those moments of pure magic when a working-class person uses their own words to describe their life.

My all-time favourite was Doreen McNally, one of the Women on the Waterfront who we interviewed during the dockers' strike. "Our roots go deep down in the belly of the Mersey and they don't pull up easily."

We would then incorporate these nuggets of actuality into the songs or scenes. There was always a visual script being projected as well, complementing or contradicting the action on stage. By the time I left we were using video recordings and the visual script had become film clips.

I had been successfully using this way of making theatre for six years with the young people in Shout! Youth Theatre Group. I was keen to try it with the women. What might be a good subject?

I had been planning to write a play commemorating the 25th anniversary of the closure of the Steel Works. Regeneration had started with a vengeance; Corby was changing, and lots of people coming to the town seemed unaware of our history. Not only that, I was concerned that the 1979 Steel Strike was not being given the prominence it deserved in working-class history, after the late Tony Benn had failed to mention it whilst recalling the big industrial disputes during a speech at the annual Chain Maker's rally which I had recently attended. That omission had left me furious. Knowing the devastation both the strike and subsequent closures had inflicted on my home town, I felt duty-bound to tell our story.

I discussed the idea with the group. Many of them had worked in the steel works and most had relatives who were steelworkers. They were really excited at the prospect and so we decided that we would work together with Shout! and tell the story of the demise of the steel industry through the voices of women and children. That way we would humanise an otherwise dry, industrial story.

Our Bodies, Ourselves was ready in a simple monologue format in time for IWD 2005, and we performed it at Corby Library. The feedback was very encouraging, so we set about expanding the material and began to work with some of the young women from Shout! to create the stage play which we later performed in August at the ARC Theatre in Corby.

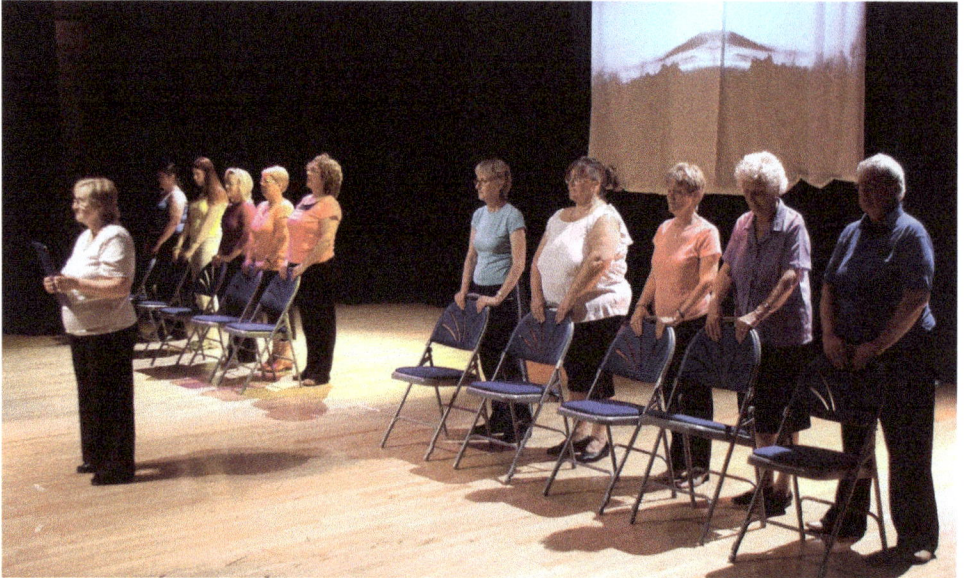

*The original cast of Our Bodies,
Ourselves at the ARC Theatre August 2005*

Women of Steel was eventually ready for performance at East Carlton Park by July 2006, running from 26th to 29th. It was a truly unique event created specifically for the venue with an unusual first act where the audience was divided into groups of ten with each group beginning their journey in a different part of the heritage centre. Actresses were in situ amongst the remnants of the steelworks to tell the story of Isa the widow, Gwenda the homesick emigree, Maureen the steelworker, cleaners, canteen workers and the growth of the town.

Following a restaging in the café of the meeting which led to the decision to strike, the audience were led out to the patio, where a re-enactment of the big ROSAC (The campaign group set up to campaign for the retention of Steel at Corby) demo took place.

The actual banners from the campaign had been loaned by Warwick University Archive, and there was a speech from Peter McGowan, who was one of the steel workers who had actually marched to London in 1979 as part of a deputation to parliament.

The audience were immersed in the demonstration and enthusiastically booed "Maggie Thatcher", who appeared with detonator and megaphone in hand. After berating the masses, she "blew up" our cardboard cut-out Corby Candle, (a well-known landmark) complete with a massive firework boom, before heading off to the marquee we had hired as the new Enterprise Zone. Accompanied by a live band, the audience followed for the second act, which involved the women sharing how they had survived after closure, the middle generation telling how they had lived through the wasted years, (before regeneration), - and the Youth Theatre sharing their hopes for the future.

Since funding was really tight, we had to sleep over in the marquee after each performance as we couldn't afford security. It was a life-changing experience for quite a few people, and firm friendships were made between the generations that have lasted till the present day. We had the event filmed and got really good reviews. We all knew that we had done Corby proud. We had honoured the past, acknowledged the present and looked hopefully to the future.

A few weeks after the event, the women arranged for us to meet up for a walk in the park. I put on my wellies and raingear and headed off to the meet-up. I was confused as to why the woman who was giving me a lift was so smartly dressed and made up.

CWThG members at East Carlton Park ready for our walk.

On arrival we headed off on the walk only to discover that in fact this was a tree-planting! The women had obtained permission for me to plant a rowan tree they had bought, and for a plaque to be put up to commemorate our play.

Paula Boulton planting the tree

When the press appeared, I realised why the women were all looking so glamorous! Unfortunately, the rowan tree didn't last – but the plaque is there and we have very solid memories of the project.

Hoping our sapling grows to this size

My thankyou gift to the women was to have been a digital presentation copy of the annotated script containing photos of the projections which had been shown behind them in the various scenes. While I was preparing it, Marian Anderson from Corby Zone, the local Arts development company which was supporting the project, had said "That's a book, Paula!" "I've never written a book," I said. "Well, Kenny knows all about desktop publishing – let's ask him!" Kenneth Martin was one of the five-strong Corby Zone team. We had the skills in-house – and before I knew it, we were off and running.

The "Wasted Years" section of the play had been written by Emma Boulton Roe, and both Kirsty Graham and Jack Boulton Roe had penned their own contributions to the Look to the Future section. They were thrilled that their work was going to be in print. The book was a real team effort and ended up with a whole new section expanding on subjects which were only casually referred to in the play.

While it was being prepared someone else asked us to restage *Women of Steel*, as due to the site-specific nature of the original play, audience numbers had been limited. So I rewrote it as an indoor stage play and, in keeping with our tradition, we performed the new version at the ARC theatre for IWD 2007. My fondest memory of the rehearsals was when one of the group, Bridie, realised that in a normal play you start at the beginning and go through in a sequence to the end. Her first experience of acting had been the East Carlton Park version of *Women of Steel,* which had required her to repeat the same scene 6 times over for groups of 10 at a time.

While the play was still fresh, and given that the theatre was available and was the perfect space, it seemed like a good idea to get a performance filmed for posterity. Rather than trying to capture a live performance, we decided to make a proper film.

So a few weekends later we were back at the ARC with a fabulous team of people covering every aspect of filming imaginable. I was there to help ensure the performances were accurate. However, when we arrived on set for the first day of filming it turned out that Rachel, the film director had phoned in sick. Now, I knew how to direct a play, but I had never directed a film. The cast however, appeared to think directing was directing and persuaded me to take her place.

We had a crazy time. Luckily Corby Zone - all young Corby graduates - knew what they were doing. And we had the expertise of our usual trusted technicians. A whole production schedule was in place, and somehow we muddled through. The stand-out experience for me was my gradual transformation into the character of Maggie Thatcher, who I had to play while continuing to direct.

Between takes I would pop out to the changing-rooms and get the next bit of the outfit on. Then the wig, then the make-up. The cast looked more and more bemused until finally it was a Maggie look-alike sitting there telling them what to do!

Then began the long and arduous process of editing. Endless glitches and endless viewings of the film – some insurmountable sound issues, a post-production nightmare for another bright Corby graduate. But eventually it was done, and we reconvened at the ARC for a fabulous red-carpet film premiere. Maggie Thatcher even put in a surprise appearance! And a full house cheered enthusiastically to see that *Women of Steel* - the film – was as much of a success as the plays had been.

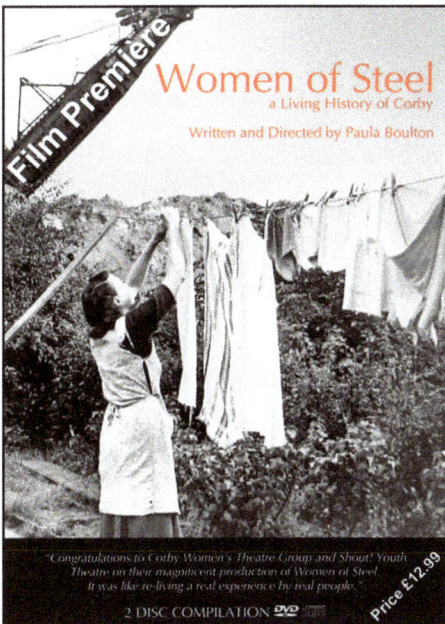

Corby Women's Theatre Group & Shout! Youth Theatre present...

Women of Steel
a Living History of Corby

Written and Directed by Paula Boulton

Film Premiere

"Congratulations to Corby Women's Theatre Group and Shout! Youth Theatre on their magnificent production of Women of Steel. It was like re-living a real experience by real people."

2 DISC COMPILATION DVD

Price £12.99

The Arc Theatre, Rockingham Road, Corby
Thursday 12th June 7.30pm

Tickets available from Rocky Road Music, £5 / £3

For more info tel. Paula on 01536 741922

CORBYZONE
www.corbyzone.org.uk

Photos of the filming and the show were expertly curated for an exhibition called *Stories of Steel* by Marian Anderson from Corby Zone, which gave us another focus whilst I continued with the book, which had been bubbling away in the background.

In that same year Emma and I created *River of Life* for Northant's Black History Association, a short, time-limited project resulting in several performances with an ad hoc cast. Several members of Corby Women's Theatre Group, keen to expand their theatrical experience, took part in this production too.

NORTHAMPTONSHIRE
Black History
ASSOCIATION

OUNDLE
FESTIVAL *of* LITERATURE

River of Life

Everyday Heroes from Northamptonshire's Black History

Directed by Paula Boulton and Emma Boulton-Roe

A multimedia community performance exploring some of the county's best kept secrets.

Tuesday 4 March 2008, 7.30pm
Queen Victoria Hall, Oundle,
Call Oundle Tourist Office 01832 274333

Monday 10 March 2008, 7.30pm
The Arc, Rockingham Road Primary, Corby, NN17 1AJ
Call Rocky Road Records 01536 203810

Tickets £3.
All enquires to Northamptonshire Black History Association,
01604 590967

Bridges
Bringing communities together through arts and celebration

CORBYZONE

Supported by
The National Lottery®
through the Heritage Lottery Fund

Heritage
Lottery Fund

The following year, 2008, we had the book launch and finally I was able to present the cast members with a thankyou gift - their own copy. Lots of the group got involved in promoting and selling the book and joining me at book signings. We learned a lot along the way, managing to shift all 1500 of the initial print-run. Corby folk had dispersed far and wide after the closure of the steelworks, so copies of *Women of Steel* followed them.

Meanwhile, Corby Women's Theatre Group had continued to meet and were onto their next project. This time Emma, who had had her first play-writing experience working with me on *Women of Steel*, asked me to be her mentor on a new play which had attracted Arts Council funding. We began collecting more stories of the women of Corby, and between us we crafted them into a script which was performed as a play-reading. *About Her* had attracted several new members to the group, in particular Danijela from Serbia and Anna from Poland. We also continued the tradition of involving women from the Women's Centre and young women from Shout! At the time I was chair of the Domestic Abuse forum and never too far away from the support networks around the survivors. We always held a collection to give to the refuge at our performances. So I was not at all surprised that domestic violence was once again a theme in *About Her*.

About Her logo based on photos of the original cast

What was more unusual was how I found my interviewees. I was sitting writing in Morrisons café one day and a passing women asked me out of curiosity what I was doing. We struck up a conversation, and before I knew it she was sharing her tale of escaping from a violent relationship. Her story later featured in *About Her,* and I well remember watching her in the audience go through a range of emotions as she heard her own tale told.

One of the most rewarding and moving aspects of this sort of theatre is to witness a woman seeing her story play out before her on stage. That truth-telling is often a really validating experience and may well be the first time she has felt heard.

The play-reading version was yet another new approach to a script. Emma and I had agreed a set of themes to explore in our interviews. We then created the characters and staged conversations between them as if they were meeting in real life. One of the stylistic aspects of Corby Women's Theatre group was having a semi-circle of chairs on stage where the women would appear to be chatting spontaneously and organically, leading to one of them stepping forward and telling her story. This material worked perfectly for that format.

The final version contained all the interviews and all the characters, so that any other group could string them together how they chose, either as a series of character's stories, or a series of reflections by those characters on the same topic.

The characters were so real that we decided they needed a chance to be on stage properly. Our Arts Council funding had run out, but we eventually raised more for me to write and produce a play based on the material we had collected. The task was to find a setting where the various characters might realistically have bumped into one another. *About Her* the stage play was finally set in the Lakeland's charity shop, which provided me with a couple of new characters, the women who ran the shop.

Three cast members on the set for About Her, the stage play.

24

Some of the monologues had been performed separately at the library as part of a Talking Books event. This gave me the idea of having the Talking Books woman come to the Lakelands to interview customers in the café.

We also involved a group of girls from Shout! who played the part of rowdy teenagers in the town centre and allowed for the older generation to comment on how life had been for them when they were that age.

The cast of About Her at the ARC Theatre 2010

Other young people were drawn into the project due to Emma having been appointed as lecturer in Performing Arts at Tresham, the local FE college. She told a whole group of textile students about the project and they created a fabulous patchwork backdrop from images of the women in their lives.

This was the beginning of a fruitful partnership with the college.

The patchwork backdrop created by textile students from Tresham

Several of us in the group had been intimately involved in getting a new women's refuge for Corby. The original one had burned down 7 years previously and we had been making do with a series of safe houses spread across the town. Many women had first-hand experience of life in refuge accommodation and had readily taken part in a creative consultation to design the ideal refuge. Seven years of negotiations as part of my work as chair of the domestic abuse forum and Co-ordinator at the Women's Centre had brought us to the point where our dream had come true.

The *About Her* performance took place at the ARC Theatre in 2010, just after we had proudly opened this new purpose-built refuge. Six individual flats giving each woman her own front door, whilst retaining the support function of having a worker on site and communal facilities all within a secure perimeter. One flat was fully adapted for wheelchair access too.

We had raised a lot of money from ticket sales and donations that night and it was a special moment to be able to present a cheque to the new refuge worker.

Managing to raise money for a real cause through our theatre work whilst shining a light on issues affecting women in working-class communities gave us all a boost. The plays had a contemporary and authentic feel, and characters were familiar – like women we knew and recognised in the community. For me as a writer I felt that I knew exactly what they would have said, their accents and vernacular were the voices around me growing up. So, it was a departure from the usual subject matter and methodology to be commissioned to write a new play, this time not a subject that we chose ourselves, nor about people alive today. I was asked to write a play which looked at the lives of women 100 years earlier, for the *Our Corby* project at the new Core theatre, using a selection of photos from the Seaborne Collection of archive photos as a starting point.

It was a challenge. No people to meet or interviews to undertake which normally allowed me to swim in the subject matter until characters and ideas floated to the surface. This time I had to imagine lives and intuit what may have been going on in an old photo; to create the story behind the image.

In addition, the commission included the opportunity to perform the piece at the *Our Corby* festival in the new all-singing and all-dancing theatre. I had been shown round and seen how the stage could be reformatted and was excited to come up with another novel structure building on the site-specific ideas behind *Women of Steel*. Also, our work had never exploited theatrical effects or fancy sound and lighting, as we were limited in our access to theatre space.

Of all the photos that I looked through, a few really stood out for me. I kept coming back to the 1911 one of the Crackers - women in bonnets and aprons wielding pickaxes which they used to break up the stones in the iron works.

Cast members from Heritage –
a Cracker with pick axe and two visitors.

Then there were also photos of the war memorial in Corby old village, the school, the traditional cottages and the big house. My background research told me about the link with the local landed gentry, and I found diary extracts which the vicar's wife had kept with tales of suffragette activities, the situation in Ireland, and the build-up to the first world war.

We had always been fortunate to have the services of the very talented set designer Jennifer Garlick. So, I decided that we would create an immersive experience for the audience, transforming the theatre into our version of Corby Heritage Centre and allowing the audience to wander amongst the re-enactors and the various exhibits.

Unfortunately, access to the theatre was in reality extremely limited, and I was told it would not be possible to have the space as I wanted it. We would have to work with the traditional set-up.

Undeterred, Jen created individual sets for each exhibit to be arranged on stage, with a plan to invite the audience to explore them at the end of the play.

All this notwithstanding, we created a quirky, entertaining and educational play, *Heritage* - complete with Lady Brudenell getting in and out of her coffin on stage,

a Cracker wielding a pickaxe, a full-scale remembrance service, ghosts haunting the Heritage Centre, a suffragette, a Victorian schoolmarm, an Irish farm-worker, a vicar's wife and a cleaner - all bringing the history of Corby to life.

It was choosing these characters that got the script started; I remember walking up and down Aberystwyth promenade figuring out how to bring them together in a play. I also had to consider who was in the theatre group at that time as possible performers. I had a particularly crazy creative conversation with my sister Rebecca – the costume mistress for the group – and somehow came up with the idea of ghosts as characters. And I also had links with a talented portrait artist who created four wonderful roller blinds based on the four ghosts. It all began to coalesce into a play.

It was well known that my productions often included other community groups and that this usually led to a large diverse audience. I was asked to make this the usual "Paula special", so I did just that. A couple of young women from Shout! joined the cast, whilst others took backstage roles and learned stage management from Jen, and hair and make-up from Cory Gray. We always built in mentoring, so I was more than happy to have Caitlin Folwell as my assistant.

But the real added value was bringing in live musicians. A string quartet played from one balcony, a recorder consort played from the other, a children's choir marched on at one point, and Corby Silver Band emerged from the audience and took over the stage for the remembrance service at the end.

Corby Silver Band performing in Heritage at the Core in 2011

Recorder Consort performing in Heritage at the Core in 2011

Anna Judge with Our Ladies choir
performing in Heritage at the Core in 2011

String Quartet performing in Heritage at the Core in 2011

I may not have got the theatre space of my dreams to create a truly immersive experience, but we certainly provided a very unusual event and gave the women of Corby Women's Theatre Group the chance to perform in a fully equipped theatre to full houses at both an evening and matinee performance in July 2011.

The cast of Heritage

As a footnote, there was a particularly humorous anecdote from the box office. The working title for *Heritage* for a while was *Crackers*. Someone had walked in and said curtly "Paula Boulton's Crackers?" The women selling tickets didn't know whether to agree or sell her a ticket!

In 2012 Shout! decided to become an intergenerational theatre group and asked to work with adults too. Many of them remembered *Women of Steel*, and so when I was asked to write a play to commemorate the founding of Corby Trades and Labour club in 2013, I invited CWThG members to be involved. *If Bricks Could Talk* was performed at the newly renovated Labour Club, where we had attracted a grant to finally install our own sound, lighting and projection equipment.

CWThG members in If Bricks Could Talk

The following year I wrote *Letters Home* for the commemoration of WW1, which again involved a mixed cast bringing together members of many local groups. This time we were in our bespoke theatre, and so could create a fully immersive experience. The audience walked in to find the War Memorial in the centre of the hall, and were invited to lay a poppy in remembrance of their loved ones. We then moved through the arc of time from WW1 around the room until we ended back at the war memorial to remember all those who had been killed in wars since "the war to end all wars".

Cast members in Letters Home

Half way through we had a mock air raid and the audience were shepherded behind a curtain into our makeshift shelter. The comments afterwards confirmed my belief in getting the audience involved. Someone pointed out that the sense of not knowing what was going to happen next added that air of suspense which is all too real in war.

The Corby Women's Theatre Group members who took part were so used to each new play offering them a completely different style that they simply adapted and played very convincing mothers, sisters, daughters and wives of those sent to the trenches in WW1.

It is important to mention that the cast for the first Corby Women's Theatre Group play in 2005 included an 80-year-old woman, Charlotte McCrorie, and a number of women in their 60s.

Sadly, twenty years on, several of our company have passed on and are no longer with us.

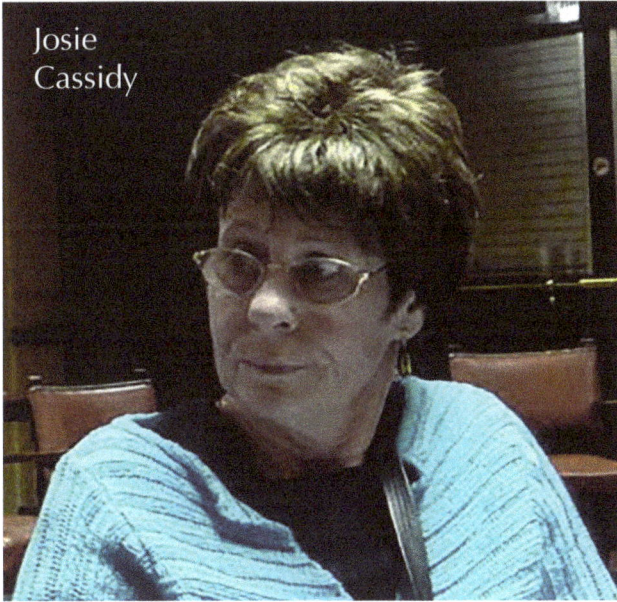
Josie Cassidy

Additionally, we lost Josie Cassidy and Joy Elizabeth Surgey to cancer, and last year, Bridie Norton, one of our octogenarians, caught Covid after struggling with her health for many years.

We remember them with fondness and heartfelt thanks for the part they played in this remarkable group of women who over a 20-year period managed to tell important stories about real lives with humility, passion and talent. For many of them this had been their first introduction to theatre or being on stage.

I am proud to have been given the chance to work with them to create such real, authentic work.

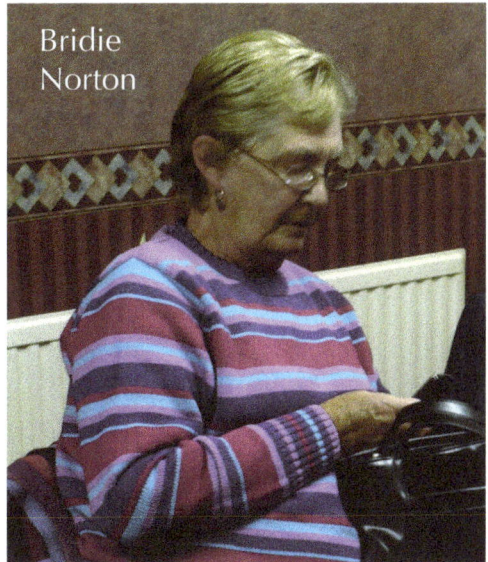
Bridie Norton

As part of the *Corby Women, Then and Now* project in 2023, we held a reunion in February to discuss who wanted to be involved in the new play. It was wonderful to reconnect with the various women who had taken part over the years. The reunion included Zoom so that Anna Judge, who now lives in Spain, could join us.

It was like any other meeting in that as soon as we sat in a circle, we were off! I mentioned another play I was writing for Worker's Memorial Day, and out poured the stories – gritty, real, moving. Stories of struggle after another 13 years of Tory rule. Life being lived around us and by us – lives worthy of documenting, and usually invisible.

That is always how the plays started. Women talking together sharing experiences which then get transformed into a play.

We are sticking with this tried and tested process to develop the new play and will be meeting with young women and girls from local schools and colleges to share our work and explore with them how women's lives have changed.

Sharing across the generations was once the cornerstone of building community. With the demise of the extended family such opportunities are rare and precious. We are excited to be able to have this chance.

Society goes to great pains to portray women's conversations as idle chatter, gossip, inconsequential. We know different. Women speaking our personal truths is a revolutionary act, capable of sowing seeds, sparking a flame, causing a ripple, rocking the boat. This is what we need to convey.

Women's herstory is largely untold and unwritten. It is up to us to pass it on in the women's way - the time-honoured oral tradition. Pulling back the curtain to reveal the reality of women's lives may inspire the next generation. Showing them their strong, capable foremothers and sharing the struggles they went through, will, we hope, encourage them to stand tall as did the crackers and the women of steel before them.

We want them to take charge of their destiny, forge their own futures, stand up and be counted, not afraid to speak up and speak out, knowing that they follow in our footsteps and are ready to pick up the baton in the never-ending fight for women's rights.

Times change, and today's young women have to develop new skills to survive in an increasingly disjointed technological society. We have much to learn from them.

The new production will be performed by a mixture of Corby women then and now, some of the young women and some members of Corby Women's Theatre Group. Could this be a new start?
Hold me back folks. There is still work to be done. Tales to tell.
Yarns to spin. And a reinvigorated Corby Women's Theatre Group might well be the one to do it.

Memorabilia
OUR BODIES OURSELVES

PEARLS

present

Corby Women's Theatre Group

in

Our Bodies Ourselves

Director: Paula Boulton

at

The Arc Theatre
Rockingham Road, Corby
on Saturday August 6th at 7.30pm

All proceeds to Corby Women's Refuge

Tickets £5.00 (£4.00)
from Rocky Road Music
01536 203810

Supported by
Workers Educational Association
and
Corby Community Arts

Corby Women's Theatre Group

in

Our Bodies Ourselves

Director: Paula Boulton

at

The Arc Theatre, Rockingham Road, Corby
on Saturday August 6th at 7.30pm

All proceeds to Corby Women's Refuge

Tickets £5.00 (£4.00)
from Rocky Road Music
01536 203810

0 3 3

OUR BODIES OURSELVES

Cast in order of appearance

Lorraine Scatterty

Joyce Stirling

Irene Hamilton

Joan Smith

Charlotte McCrorie

Lesley Trout

Betty McPherson

Lola Dziarkowska

Barbara Hawthorn

Jen Ross

Linda Kilpatrick

Paula Boulton

Una Caulfield

WOMEN OF STEEL

Corby Women's Theatre Group
& Shout! Youth Theatre
present

WOMEN OF STEEL

"I would like to dedicate this play to inspirational comrades who led their lives believing they could make a difference!"

at East Carlton Park

July 27th
July 28th
July 29th
7.30pm

Programme

Written, directed and produced by
Paula Boulton
with assistance from Emma Boulton Roe

About the Play - Content

The play has been created and performed to look at where we are 25 years since the Steel Work closure, honour the struggle to Save Steel and acknowlege the fact that hard working people have come to Corby from all over the world for 70 years. Sharing our rich history with the new Corby people will show them they can be proud of the town they have chosen to live in, and join us in looking to a great future.

About the Play - Style

The play is a unique, multi -media, site specific event where the audience move around live exhibits in the heritage centre. Drama, visual image, voice montage and live music are interwoven to tell the true stories of the Women of Steel and the Ore Kids who lived through these turbulent times.

Performers and people

Corby Women's Theatre group formed in September 2004 to do this play. Originally the group was funded as an evening class by the Workers Educational association ,which enabled Paula to share the entire process of " Creating a community Drama". Over 25 women have been part of the group at some stage , and all have contributed their life experience to the process.

Shout! Youth Theatre was formed in 1998 by Paula and Emma. All 4 younger women are former members of Shout!. The group regularly create unique pieces of theatre as commissioned. Earlier this year they toured Northamptonshire libraries with their play about teenage pregnancy "To Do Or Not to Do" If you are interested in joining either group contact Paula on 01536 741922

Our guest performers are all former steel workers who walked to London with the Save Steel petition.

We are proud to welcome Emma Boulton Roe to the project. Born in 1980, Emma is a newly returned Performing Arts graduate and she wrote the section of the play which looks at how it was to grow up in Corby since Steel.

Performers

Shout! Youth Theatre

Joris Alexander
Georgia Britton
Robert Cain
John Connelly
Lee Docherty
Tony Giles
Kirsty Graham
Philip Jennings
Terri Langley
Jodie Mallett
Kirsty O'Neil
Amy Pointer
Jennifer Pyper
Jack Boulton Roe
Danielle Skillen
Leanne Villette
Shareace White

Corby Women's Theatre Group

Jo Alderson
Danielle Boulton
Betty Brown
Josie Cassidy
Lorraine Dziarkowska
Irene Hamilton
Betty MacPherson
Margaret Marshall
Bridie Norton
Emma Boulton Roe
Jennifer Ross
Lorraine Scatterty

With guest appearances from:
Mark Conway and
Crystal Dziarkowska

Steel Men: John Cowling
Jim McDonald
Peter McGowan
John Forshaw

The Ore Bits

Paula Boulton	Violin and vocals
Ian Cameron	Vocals
Alan Hewitt	Whistle, percussion and vocals
Benita Hewitt	Accordion and Flute
Clive Parker	Banjo and percussion
George Reilly	Guitar and vocals
Emma Boulton Roe	Guitar and vocals
Rebecca Boulton Roe	Vocals
With Jack Boulton Roe	Drum

Act One

The play unfolds in many locations. Please stay with your groups and your stewards will guide you. The scenes can be viewed in any order.

Café
Roots

Works

- **Jobs May Come** 🎵
- **Reservoir Song** 🎵
- **Morgan Squire** 🎵
- **In the Shadow of the Works 2000**
by *Emma Boulton Roe*

- **My Home 2000**
by *Emma Boulton Roe*

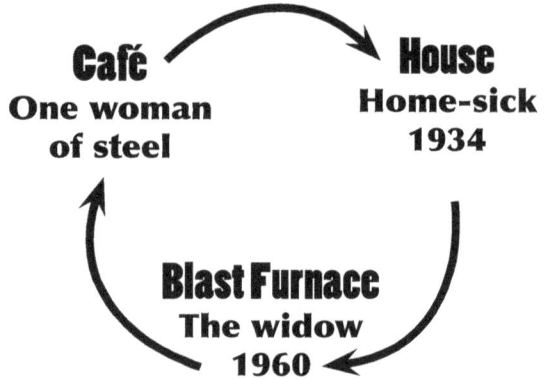

Café
One woman
of steel

House
Home-sick
1934

Blast Furnace
The widow
1960

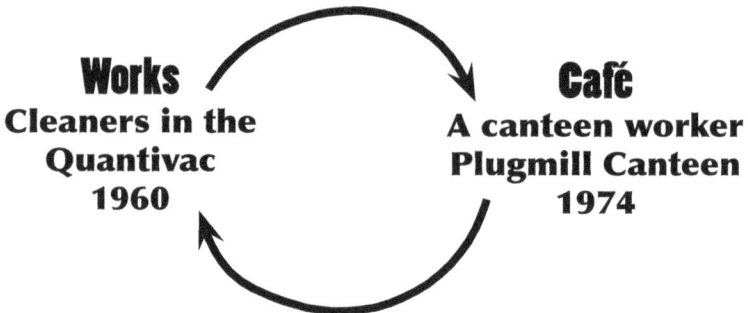

Works
Cleaners in the
Quantivac
1960

Café
A canteen worker
Plugmill Canteen
1974

Café

- **As the work grows, so the town goes** 🎵
- **Canteen 1979 Union meeting**

Patio

- **R.O.S.A.C. demonstration**
- **The end of steel**

Act Two

Outside
Wonder World Calypso ♫

Please follow the Pied Piper of Wonderworld to the marquee

Marquee

Era *Wonderworld Wonderwhen? 1984*
- **Broken Dreams**
- **The Aftermath**
- **Stand Your Ground**
- **Goodbye to Wonderworld 1990**

Era *Wasted Years 1990 - 2005*
- **Asbury's Chocolate Factory 1998**
  by *Emma Boulton Roe*

Era *The Present Day* ⇨
- **Steel Kids**
- **The Future**
- **Our Reality**
- **I wish**
  by Kirsty Graham
- **Til the end**
  by Jack Boulton Roe and Tony Giles
- **A cut above**
  by the performers
- **Hope for the future**
- **Give us a chance** ♫

The End

Music

Village Life	Orebits
Keep the Candle Burning	Mike Carver
Happy Town of Steel (words and music)	Bobby Civil
Sweatshop and *Broken Dreams*	Banner Theatre
Wonderworld	Ian Cameron
Old Corby Song	handed down by Mary King to her daughter Ann Brown

All other songs written and composed by the OREBITS for **It Starts With the Ore** in 1985.

N.B.　All of the songs tonight are available on CD.
　　　　Contact Emma tel: 01536 262054

Creative Team

Costume Mistress	Rebecca Boulton Roe
Set Design& construction	Marian Anderson with Jenny Garlick
Poster design	Lyn Plumpton, Jan Timmins
Programme design	Corby Community Arts
Dialect coach	Maggie Marshall
Visual Script	Lorraine Dziarkowska community photographer.
Assistants	Lyn Plumpton , JanTimmins With James Steventon & Marian Anderson

Access to the ET library has been invaluable. Liz McBride, thanks for her co-operation. East Carlton Park for providing copies of their archive material. Kevin Hayes for training. The images have been researched from a wide variety of places and many from my own collection, a real community spirit, many thanks to all who contributed. Apologies to those who have not been acknowledged personally.

Technical Crew

Technical Manager	Nick Maple
Technical assistants	Andrew Maple
Video editing	Sami Scott with Professional Video Productions and Andy Eathorne
Sound editing & projection	Sami Scott
Film Crew	Ellie Morton and Professional Video productions

Venue & stage management
Joyce Stirling

Administration
Jo Alderson, Lorraine scatterty, Lyn plumpton

Front of house team
Joyce Stirling with Daisy Dziarkowska

Research
Thanks to John Wood Cowling, Jim McDonald, Peter McGowan, John Forshaw, Frank Smythe, Mick McGowan, Aiden Coleman, Jane Carr, Peter Floody, Norman

Interviewees
Jean Hall, Winnie Scott, Anne-Marie Lawson, Maureen Forshaw, Betty MacPherson, Lorraine Dziarkowska, Joyce Stirling, Carol Lowe, Stanley Boulton, Eda Wood, Shirley White, Rachel Arnold, Sami Scott, the cast and past members of CWTHG.

How it happened
"I finally got the funding for the bulk of this project in Dec 2005, 18 months after I started! I was ready to give up at that point. The anniversary year had come and gone and my enthusiasm was waning! Until a walk in East Carlton Park and the memory of a wonderful outdoor event collided and I was off again with the idea of writing the play around the heritage centre! Thanks to Jack, Sue and Emma who pushed me to do it, and the women of steel who have stuck with it throughout. I believe between us all we have created something unique which has taken on a life of its own."

Paula Boulton

Thanks

This whole project has been a great team effort. Many people have contributed time and energy to make it a reality. Too many to list. But especial thanks to Pete Rob, Aiden Coleman and the staff of East Carlton Park, Peter Floody, The Lighthouse, Rotraut Anderson, Bob Chapman for sharing the vision, Madelyn McAlpine, CBC print room, Pete Weston, Ruth Tindley, Rockingham Primary School for stage blocks, Ken Penton from Community trade union for the loan of the ISTC banner, Eammon Norton, Corby Trades and Labour club for rehearsal venue, Julie Steventon and Val Stein for script critique and editing, our bus drivers Rein, Lisa and Alan, our Stewards.

Corby Women's Refuge

Any proceeds from the performances will go to the new Corby Women's Refuge. About the refuge: Corby, the town with the highest rate of Domestic Violence in the county has been without a refuge since 2000. Several of CWTHG are involved in establishing a new one. This is our chosen charity. The new refuge is now in planning stage and will hopefully be open within a year.

Men of Steel

Paula's next project looks at the men's experience of the Steel works. If you wish to contribute, please contact Paula on 01536 741922.

Sponsors

An anonymous donor who believes in the future of Corby
Corus
Stagecoach

Funded by

Corby Women's Theatre Group
& Shout! Youth Theatre present

Women of Steel

Thurs 8th and Fri 9th March 2007
7.30pm @ The Arc Theatre
Rockingham Road, Corby

Written & Directed by
Paula Boulton
with assistance from
Emma Boulton Roe

Programme 50p

About the Play

This multimedia theatre adaptation of Women Of Steel was written in response to the requests from people who missed the original outdoor production. Women Of Steel was written to commemorate the closure of the Steel works in Corby in 1980. Through the eyes of women, the play looks at the first influx of new communities in the 30's and takes us through the heyday of Steel production, the battle to Save Steel, the Wonderworld of the 80's, and the depression of the middle years, and concludes with the promise of regeneration, as seen through the eyes of young people.

Playwright and director Paula Boulton says "In writing the play I wanted to look at where we are 25 years since closure, honour the struggle to Save Steel, and acknowledge the fact that hard working people have come to Corby from all over the world for 70 years. Sharing our rich history with the new Corby people will show them they can be proud of the town they have chosen to live in, and join us in looking to a great future."

Performers and People

Corby Women's Theatre Group formed in September 2004 to create this play, which was first staged at East Carlton Park in July 2006.

Originally the group was funded in an evening class by the Workers Educational Association, which enabled Paula Boulton to share the entire process of 'creating a community drama'. Over 25 women have been part of the group at some stag, and have all contributed their life experiences to the process.

Shout! Youth Theatre was formed in 1998 by Paula Boulton and Emma Boulton Roe. Both younger women are former members of Shout! and Emma wrote the section of the play that looks at how it was to grow up in Corby since steel. Shout! regularly creates unique pieces of theatre as commissioned, such as their play about teenage pregnancy, 'To Do Or Not To Do' which they toured around Northamptonshire libraries.

If you are interested in joining either group, please contact Paula on 01536 741 922

Our guest performers are former steel workers who walked to London with the Save Steel petition.

How it happened

"I finally got the funding for the bulk of this project in December 2005, 18 months after I started! I was ready to give up at that point. The anniversary year had come and gone and my enthusiasm was waning! Until a walk in East Carlton Park and the memory of a wonderful outdoor event collided and I was off again with the idea of writing the play around the heritage centre! Thanks to Jack, Sue and Emma who pushed me to do it, and the women of steel who have stuck with it throughout. I believe between us all we have created something unique which has taken on a life of its own."   *Paula Boulton July 2006*

When Women Of Steel was staged in East Carlton Park in July 2006 it totally sold out, so even though Paula felt she was ready to move on to something new, public and peer pressure mounted for Women Of Steel to happen again.

Corby Women's Theatre Group as a whole felt compelled to offer the play to a wider audience and to present a more enduring version of their creation to the town for future generations.

Paula joined forces with Marian Anderson to seek funding for a wider project 'Stories of Steel' that includes this adaptation of the play for The Arc Theatre and will create of a series of archive materials that will last beyond the actual theatre production.

The launch of the visual and digital archive will take place later this year. A pre-order form is included in this programme so you can express your interest in these items early.

Research

Thanks to John Wood Cowling, Jim McDonald, Peter McGowan, John Forshaw, Frank Smythe, Mick McGowan, Aidan Coleman, Jane Carr, Peter Floody and Norman Coates.

Interviewees

Jean Hall, Winnie Scott, Anne-Marie Lawson, Maureen Forshaw, Betty MacPherson, Lorraine Dziarkowska, Joyce Stirling, Carol Lowe, Stanley Boulton, Eda Wood, Shirley White, Rachel Arnold, Sami Scott, the cast and past members of Corby Women's Theatre Group.

Performers

Shout! Youth Theatre

Joris Alexander
Georgia Britton
Robert Cain
Lee Docherty
Tony Giles
Kirsty Graham
Philip Jennings
Terri Langley
Jodie Mallett
Kirsty O'Neil
Amy Pointer
Jennifer Pyper
Jack Boulton Roe
Danielle Skillen
Leanne Villette
Shareace White

Corby Women's Theatre Group

Jo Alderson
Paula Boulton
Lorraine Dziarkowska
Irene Hamilton
Betty MacPherson
Margaret Marshall
Kim McGowan
Bridie Norton
Emma Boulton Roe
Jennifer Ross
Lorraine Scatterty
Julie Steventon
Joy Elizabeth Sugery
with guest appearances from:
Crystal Dziarkowska
Steel Men: Peter McGowan
                    W 'Monty' Monteith

Organisational Team

Stage Manager	Jenny Garlick
Assistant Stage Manager	Sue Rainbow
Front of House Team	Jack Boulton Roe, Louise Boyle, Micha Davis, Crystal Dziarkowska, Leanne Villette
Project Manager	Marian Anderson

Creative & Technical Team

Costume	Rebecca Boulton Roe
Props & Set	Jenny Garlick
Programme Design	Corby Community Arts & Marian Anderson
Visual Script	Lorraine Dziarkowska, Sami Scott Andy Eathorne & Paula Boulton
Technical assistants	Nick Maple & Andrew Maple
Sound editing and projection	Sami Scott
Video editing	Sami Scott with Andy Eathorne & PVP
Videographer	Joy Oliver
Photographers	Kenny Martin & Rein Kybarsepp

Music

All of the songs from this performance are available on CD, most are from
It Starts With The Ore produced in 1985
Banner Theatre – Sweatshop & Broken Dreams
Ian Cameron - Wonderworld

Act 1

Village Life

Roots

Home Sick 1934

The Widow 1960

One Woman Of Steel

Cleaners in the Quantivac 1960

A canteen worker plugmill canteen 1974

As the works grows, so the town grows

Canteen union meeting 1979

R.O.S.A.C. demonstration

The end of steel

Interval – refreshments available

Act 2

Wonderworld Wonderwhen?

Broken Dreams

The Aftermath

Stand Your Ground

Goodbye to Wonderworld

Act 3

Steel Kids

The Wasted Years

Hope for the Future

The End

Time-line for the closure of the steel works in Corby
(from the Evening Telegraph 09.02.2004)

February 1979
With 5,500 jobs under threat, it emerges there are just 60 job vacancies at the Job Centre.

Steelworkers and their families lobby then Tory-controlled Corby Council in protest at being charged for action committee meetings at the Festival Hall.

The council is accused of not doing enough to stop the closure, despite sending a delegation to the government.

April 1979
Mass rally held at the Festival Hall organised by ROSAC – the campaign for the Retention Of Steelmaking At Corby.

Total job losses predicted to be as many as 12,000.

June 1979
Thirty steelworkers and union leaders, including former council chairman Peter McGowan and former Mayor John Wood-Cowling set off on an 80-mile Jarrow-style crusade to London.

Six days later, they were joined by 400 people and travelled down from Corby for a rally around central London and a 10,000-signature petition was handed in to the House of Commons.

At the Iron and Steel Trades Confederation (ISTC) British Steel boss Sir Charles Villiers gives the clearest hint that nothing will stop the axe form falling.

Corby people feature in a documentary about how the closure will affect their lives.

A huge illuminated Save Our Steel sign is erected on top of the Strathclyde Hotel.

July 1979
British Steel challenges union bosses to come up cash saving ideas as an alternative to closure.

Corby Council appoints a jobs supremo, charged with attracting new jobs to the town.

The new Tory government, led by Margaret Thatcher, promises to keep a close eye on the negotiations.

August 1979
Shadow industry secretary John Silkin visits Corby on a fact-finding mission.

A Corby delegation meets former Labour premier Jim Callaghan in London.

September 1979
Talks between British Steel and the ISTC in Corby are disrupted by 10,000 people taking to the streets.

There are scuffles between protestors and the police. No arrests were made.

October 1979
One thousand extra police are drafted in as Corby readies itself for the expected closure announcement on November 1st.

British Steel has urgent talks with the government claiming the corporation is losing 10m a week.

November 1979
Announcement made that the steel works will close in a year's time. Corby Council applies to the government and the EEC for grants. Eventually £300m is given.

ISTC and other unions vow to continue their fight against closure.

December 1979
British Steel offers steelworkers a 2% pay rise, which eventually leads to a national strike.

Splits between union members begin to appear. Two thousand engineers vote for shutdown and a decent redundancy package, as do about 1,200 blast furnacemen. 6,000 ISTC members accept the inevitable closure.

January 1980
National steel strike over pay begins, but some Corby workers turn up for work, anxious not to jeopardise redundancy pay.

February 1980
Glebe coke ovens close. Seven hundred maintenance workers let go and 1,500 workers from the minerals and preparation plant and a major blast furnace are given notice.

National strike continues.

March 1980
The average Corby family is living on £24 a week. Blast furnacemen demand answers about strike pay, but there are clashes with strike supporters outside the Festival Hall.

April 1980
Twelve-week strike ends as steelmakers accept 15.5% pay offer.

Redundancies were phased throughout 1980.

The last steel was made on April 22nd.

Stories of Steel

Women Of Steel is part of a wider project funded by Awards For All which includes this theatre adaptation of Women Of Steel and a series of archive materials. If you require any info contact:
Marian Anderson **07946 576 977 marian.anderson@yahoo.co.uk**

Tribute

We would like to take this opportunity to pay tribute to Richard Carr, NALGO shop steward, and one of the men who walked to London with the Save Steel petition, who was killed tragically earlier this year.

Corby Women's Refuge

We will be collecting for Corby Women's Refuge on the nights of the play. Corby, the town with the highest rate of domestic violence in the county has been without a refuge since 2000. Several of Corby Women's Theatre group are involved in establishing a new one. This is our chosen charity. The new refuge is now in planning stage and will hopefully be open within a year.

Thanks

This whole project has been a great team effort. Many people have contributed time and energy to make it a reality – too many people to list. Thanks to Rocky Road Music for being our official ticket outlet, Bob Chapman for sharing the vision, The Lighthouse, Pete Weston, Ruth Tindley, Rotraut Anderson, Corby Trades & Labour Club for rehearsal venue, Julie Steventon and Val Stein for script critique and editing, Jim McClellan & Anne Hanratty at Rockingham Road Primary School/The Arc Theatre, Kingswood Church, Joy Elizabeth Sugery, Liz McBride, ET archivist, East Carlton Park Heritage Centre for providing copies of their archive material, FORTAC for administrative support, Corby Borough Council for printing the programme and Corby Women's Theatre Group for matched funding.

Supported by
The National Lottery®
through Awards for All

AWARDS FOR ALL

THE ARC

FORTAC
FEDERATION OF RESIDENTS AND
TENANTS ASSOCIATIONS CORBY

Corby
Borough Council

ABOUT HER

CORBY WOMEN'S THEATRE GROUP

presents

ABOUT HER

by

Emma Boulton Roe
Paula Boulton

CORBY WOMEN'S THEATRE GROUP

Directed by

PAULA BOULTON

Presents the first play reading of this specially, and repeatedly abridged version, of

ABOUT HER

Cast

Anne Harvey	Catherine
Anna Kolodziejska Judge	Kat
Betty McPherson	Morag
Bridie Norton	Bernadette
Chelsea McClintock	Laura
Danijela Bastajiec	Milica
Jennifer Ross	Karen
Josie Cassidy	Gaida
Joy Elizabeth Surgey	Irmgard
Kirti Karsandas	Indu
Krystina Farrell	Eva/Pauline
Linda Hallam	Ada
Lorraine Scatterty	Alma
Margaret Kavanagh	Bronagh
Sheila Royce	Helen
Tracey Keogh	Linda

About her was written by Emma Boulton Roe and Paula Boulton and is based on documentary interviews with twenty three Corby women. With the help of your feedback, we aim to produce a theatre version for International Women's Day, March 2010, at the Arc Theatre.

Transcribers: Jack Boulton Roe, Jennifer Ross, Chris Ward

Crew: Jennifer Garlick, Jan Timmins

Production Assistants: Emma Boulton Roe, Jennifer Ross

Production Consultant: Sami Scott

Advisor and evaluation: Maggie Saxon

Special thanks to our critical readers, Sheila Royce our editor, Corby Trades and Labour Club and the interviewees for sharing their stories.

Funded by Arts Council England and KCAP

LOTTERY FUNDED

Corby Women's Theatre Group Presents:

About her...

By Paula Boulton and Emma Boulton Roe

More true tales from the Women of Corby.
Ever wonder about the stories on the faces of the people passing by?
The lives behind the masks we wear?

Come and spend a day with us "up town" and discover the fascinating
lives of women you might walk past every day.

**Friday 12th and Saturday 13th March, 7:30pm,
The Arc Theatre, Rockingham Road, Corby**

Tickets £5 Available from Rocky Road Music and The Lakelands Hospice Emporium

For more info call Paula on 01536 741922

LOTTERY FUNDED   Northamptonshire
                        County Council   Corby

Corby Women's Theatre Group
'About Her'
Directed by Emma Boulton-Roe & Paula Boulton

Cast

Abby Burns	Girl
Anna Judge	Katerina
Betty McPherson	Morag
Bridie Norton	Bernadette
Caitlin Folwell	Girl
Carol Davie	Ada
Danjela Bastajic	Milica
Elicia Phillips	Girl
Elle Stephenson	Girl
Helen Cain	Girl
Jennifer Ross	Karen
Josie Cassidy	Gaida
Krystyna Farrell	Patrice
Margeret Kavanagh	Bronagh
Moira Reid	Maggie
Pat Clarke	Catherine
Sheila Royce	Alma
Tracy Keogh	Linda

Cast Liason
Lorraine Scatterty

Consultants
Maggie Saxon
Sami Scott

Lights and Sound Technician
Sami Scott

Writers
Emma Boulton-Roe
Paula Boulton

Set Designer and Stage Management
Jennifer Garlick

Production Assistant
Emma Boulton-Roe
Jennifer Ross

Assistant Stage Manager
Sue Rainbow

Special Thanks to the Corby Trades and Labour Club, The ARC Theatre, Turnabout, RS Components, KCAP and the interviewees that gave their stories.

HERITAGE

If you enjoyed Women of Steel or About her...
...book a ticket for Corby Women's Theatre Groups' latest & greatest local production.

Written & directed by Paula Boulton, Heritage is a specially commissioned new play, part of the 'OUR CORBY' project, inspired by Malcolm Seaborne's Photographs of Corby's history & its many diverse & eccentric characters. Suffragettes, countesses, pickaxe-wielding women of the first world war, school marms & a whole social club of argumentative ghosts all find a place in this visual, musical, comic, dramatic extravaganza.

Performed by the renowned Corby Women's Theatre Group, with guests & musicians from the local community.

Heritage is a play about Corby, not to be missed.

Saturday 23rd July 7.30pm Sun 24th July 2pm
Tickets available from The Core box office £8 /£6
For more info contact Paula on 07892489163

About the play

'Heritage' is a specially commissioned play for the 'Our Corby' project. The play was inspired by the many diverse and eccentric characters Paula encountered during her research and Malcolm Seaborne's photographs of Corby's history gave the creative team a template to work from. 'Heritage' looks at how we record and remember our History and tells us about Corby 100 years ago.

Paula worked closely with set designer Jenny Garlick to create an authentic looking Heritage Centre which you are invited to look round after the show. The rest of the creative team's designs, work together to give us a sense of what 100 years ago looked and sounded like.

On principal the company work with Corby's own - recognizing the wealth of talent our town has to offer. The musicians too have all lived or worked in Corby.

Creative Team

Paula Boulton	Writer/Director
Chelsea McClintock	Director's Assistant
Jenny Garlick	Set Design/Construction
Lorraine Scatterty	Visual Script
Mark Brennan	Soundtrack
Helen Mckay	Portrait Painter
Rebecca Boulton Roe	Costume Design
Jean Sumpter	Wardrobe Assistant
Cory Gray	Hair & Make Up
Dannie Boulton	Graphic Designer

Crew

Jenny Garlick	Stage Manager
Sue Rainbow	Assistant Stage Manager
Tim Collier	Roadie
Geoff Hirsch	Roadie/Rehearsal Crew
Andy Eathorne	DVD maker, video
Gary Hickman	Technician
Will Allen	Technician
Margaret Marshall	Photography
Daniel Murphy	Runner

Production and Admin

Paula Boulton	Producer
Caitlin Folwell	Assistant to Producer
Jennifer Ross	Administration
Chelsea McClintock	Promotions
Margaret Marshall	Cast Welfare/Finance

Musicians

Dave Ashby	Bugler

Recorder Consort
Jane Arthurs
Jonathan Mack
Judith Mack

String Quartet

Walter Jones	First Violin
Mike Gosling	Second Violin
Catherine Jeffs	Viola
Janet Crew	Cello

Our Lady of Walsingham Catholic Primary School Choir

Anna Judge	Choir Conductor
Coral Phillips	Choir Chaperone

Corby Silver Band

Music

Nana was a Suffragette
Composed & Sung by Jules Gibb
March of the Women
by Ethel Smyth
On the Beautiful Blue Danube
by J.Strauss
Pavane
by William Byrd
Bonny Sweet Robin
by John Munday

Meet the cast...

Anna Partyka Judge
Lady Adeline/
Choir Mistress

Betty McPherson
Morag the Cleaner

Bridie Norton
Farm Women/
Ghost

Carol Davie
War Memorial Women

Chelsea McClintock
Steph

Elicia Phillips
Sally

Fliss Blockley
Nana

Geoff Hirsch
Removal Man

Maggie Wood
Jessica Clarke/
Ghost of Countess

Sami Scott
Youth Worker/
Ghost of Suffragette

Sheila Royce
Cracker

Tim Collier
Removal Man

Tracy Keogh
School Marm/
Ghost

Val Moore
Archivist

Jonathan Mack
Voice of Rev Bartlett

Judith Mack
Voice of Jessica Clarke

A big thank you to:
A. Abbott & Sons, Billy Dalziel, Chris Owen, Colin Bradshaw, Corby Library Librarians, Corby Trades and Labour Club - rehearsal space, Danesholme Community Church, Darren Abel, Deanna Allen, Emma Boulton Roe for critique, Helen Mckay, James Broderick, Joel Stickley for support, Joy Elizabeth Surgey, Brenda Easton - Understudying, Margaret Kavanagh, Pat Clark, Marie Brennan, Chris Jeffries, Margaret Marshall - research and devising, Michael - Ramsey Rural Museum, Our Corby team, Peter Hill for research, Rebecca Boulton for creative ideas & The Core at the Corby Cube, especially Adam Broom.

Corby Women's Theatre Group have produced 5 new plays and a film about Corby since 2005. If you would like to join the group contact Paula on 07892489163.

AND FINALLY
A special thanks to our Corby based
Graphic Designer Dannie Boulton
danniebdesigns@hotmail.com
07886908497

Contact Paula Boulton for information on photo credits.

Our Bodies Ourselves
by
Paula Boulton

**First performed at the ARC Theatre,
Corby, on 6th August 2005**

Synopsis

Through a series of natural group conversations, poems and short scenes, a group of nine older women and three younger women explore how they feel about their bodies, social pressures around body image, what it means to be female, and aspects of reproduction, contraception and birth. They also look at ageing and how fashions and behavioural expectations around dating and social life have changed over time.

Notes for the Director

The play consists of a mixture of poems (anonymous, written by cast members and well-known), natural dialogue between the cast as themselves sharing their experiences, and short scenes where the same women play multiple characters.

It was performed by nine women aged 45 to 80 and three younger women in their early 20s. The women selected the poems they wanted to recite.

Staging and Set

The original set had an area front of curtain for individual recitation, and then on the stage itself, a semi-circle of chairs stage right where the women sat for the natural conversations. Several scenes needed sets - they are described in the script.

Characters in Order of Appearance

Nine women who play themselves discussing various topics, read poems individually or with others, and become the attendees at the Food Lovers' group and then the gym/Tai Chi session. They also perform the ensemble piece to "The Mountains are Moving".

Sauna Sketch

Maud: Older lady, quite proper, introducing her friend to local sauna

Audra: Fancies herself as better than the rest. From out of town

Pearl: Polite, chatty local woman. Proud of Corby

Gertie: Uncouth down-to-earth Glaswegian woman

Marge: A woman with alopecia

Contraception

Cath: A 15-year-old girl who makes sensible decisions about contraception but ends up getting pregnant and having an abortion

Lisa: A 15-year-old who wants to leave school early and has some risky sexual experiences

Birth Memories

Alice: An older woman who was forced to have her child adopted after getting pregnant through rape

Kayleigh: A 16-year-old pregnant girl who has a caesarean

Midwife: Assists at Kayleigh's birth

Consultant: Delivers Kayleigh's baby

Motherhood

New mother

Gran

Neighbour

Food Lovers' Group

Joyce: Food Lovers' group leader

Selina: Gym teacher with bulimia

Tiffany: Cosmetic surgery enthusiast and model

Old Age Sketch

Carer: Sympathetic carer in an old people's care home

Carer 2:   Unsympathetic carer in an old people's care home

Freda: Elderly resident wanting to share her life story

ACT ONE

Scene 1: The Pearls

*Four **Women** enter and speak in unison as a welcome to the audience.*

We are the Pearls, awfully nice girls
Here to confuse you, delude you, amuse you
To stir your emotions and get your devotion
We're learning how to act and that's a fact
Our aim to entertain we hope not in vain!
So here we go, on with the show!

***All** exit.*

The following four poems are solo pieces - the first one written by Paula Boulton and the other three by Betty McPherson.

My Body

I gaze in the mirror. What do I see?
This thing called my body looks back at me
I'm in it, they tell me, for three score and ten
This house for my spirit, and so until then
I'd better start realising just what it is
Healthy and working with nothing amiss

My skin covers all of me, holds me all in,
The bones and the organs, my face and my chin
Inside there are vessels through which my blood flows
Pumped by my heart from my head to my toes
It bends and it stretches, gets up and down
That's joints, muscles, ligaments turn me around.
The lungs which draw breath in, they keep me alive
A digestive system, which helps me to thrive

By chewing and mashing the food in my tum
Then sends what it can't use to leave by my bum
Well-padded, that's useful, it helps me to sit
Though I'm meant to be worried when those jeans don't fit

Which brings me quite well to the lines and the curves
Which pleasure the eye - they're not just for perves
A changeable layer of blubber inside
For warmth and my shapeliness to which I'm tied
There are parts of this body I use more than most
My fingers make music and open the post
My legs walk for miles over mountain and dale
In all sorts of weathers, through rain and through hail.

And inside my head is the brain, so they say
To think with, create with, work out who to pay
It gives me five senses - to see and to touch
To smell, and to listen, and taste - oh! so much
So, what is it here in the mirror I see?
I'll tell you quite simply -
THIS BODY IS ME!

My Body

There are things about my body
My so-called personal traits
They are in fact the very things
I really really hate

For instance, take my hair
I'd rather I had none
It never looks the way it should
Even when it's done
Sometimes it is wavy
Sometimes it is straight
It's one of the many parts
Of my body that I hate.

Hormones

A part of our bodies we can't even see
Is hormones, of which women never are free
We get up one morning full of life
By midday we want to end our life
Men haven't got a clue what we women go through
A sense of humour is essential
To help us through when we're premenstrual
Moods and bloating and a sense of floating
But suddenly everything's all right -
A box of chocolates is in sight.

My Eyes

I love my eyes
They are a wonderful thing
They allow us to see everything
All animals in the zoo
And also help us see the loo
They help us read our books
And also view our looks
They also help us see our way
Even on the darkest day
No matter their colour
Brown, blue, green or haze
Without them we would be
Severely disabled.

Scene 2: Sauna Sketch

This scene was devised by the cast.

MUSIC: RELAXING SPA MUSIC

SET: A table with two chairs on stage right; an open-fronted sauna cabin with two levels of benches stage left.

COSTUME: The five **Women** are in towels and/or dressing-gowns and flip-flops.

Maud and Audra are seated at the table relaxing with drink. Audra is from out of town and Maud has brought her to the sauna for the first time. Pearl is in the sauna preening and relaxing. Maud and Audra go back in to the sauna cabin, talking about going on a cruise and colours of clothes.

All	*Improvise greetings and introductions.*
Audra	*Improvises about the fact that she likes to be called Audra, she's going on a cruise, has had colours done (as if no-one heard the first time). She says she is feeling a bit nervous about being in a sauna in Corby. Has had plenty of saunas of course, but never used a public one before.*
Pearl	*(Reassuringly:)* Corby's reputation is totally untrue. You have no need to worry anyway - here at the sauna we are all very friendly and kind.

Enter Gertie, fresh from the swimming pool. She is a Glaswegian woman, who is quite annoyed.

Gertie	Bastards, I'm sure them kids are pishing' in the soddin' pool. Ma eyes are pure stinging even with these glasses on. I don't know why these women come to the bloody pool when all they want tae dae is talk. Up and doon taking up the body width of the pool, three a-fuckin'-breast. Not a thought for any other poor bastard that needs tae get rid o' their anger through vigorous exercise. (*She drops her goggles and bends down, giving **Audra** a full-on view of her generous backside. **Audra** is shocked but **Gertie** doesn't notice a thing*)
Pearl	Hey Gertie, this here is Audra, I was just telling her what a friendly bunch we are here.
Gertie	Oh hello, nice tae meet ya, excuse ma French Audra. No Marge the day?
Pearl	Says she's a sore back. Poor Marge. I'm a martyr to my back.

*Sympathetic response from **Others**, who have a discussion about backs.*

Gertie	Poor Marge my arse! Excuse the French. You know why they call her Marge? Because she spreads it aboot.

*Enter **Marge**.*

Pearl	Talk of the devil!

Awkward silence.

83

Pearl	*(Starts rubbing sugar on her legs:)* Anyone for sugar? *(Others look surprised.)* Sugar. It's good for the skin.
Audra	Oh, you mean an exfoliant.
Pearl	You're welcome to try it, works a treat to get all the dead skin off.
Audra	Thank you, but I have some Helena Rubinstein. *(Notices **Gertie**'s legs:)* I see you are waiting for a waxing. Isn't it awful having to look like a gorilla before they can wax you?
Gertie	Oh fuck no - scuse ma French. I canny be daeing wi' all that fussing aboot.
Audra	Terribly unhygienic though, wouldn't you say?
Gertie	Nothing unhygienic aboot that! *(Proffers **Audra** her hairy armpit:)* Here, get a whiff o' that an' tell me if you can smell a thing!
Audra	*(Horrified, turns away, sees **Marge**'s legs and smiles:)* You're nice and smooth - what do you use?
Marge	Alopecia.
Pearl	Can you get that in Boots?
Gertie	It's an illness, stupid.

Pearl	Oh, sorry.
Marge	*(Unfazed:)* My hair fell out through stress!
Gertie	*(Looks intrigued:)* Everywhere? *(To **Maud**:)* Have you still got hairs doon there?
Pearl	Gertie, mind your own business, you're embarrassing Maud.
Gertie	Sorry hen, I didnae mean to be rude, no offence an' that. I was just thinking of a lassie in the Labour Club on Saturday night. Came back from the lavs all glum-looking 'cos she'd just found her first grey hair doon there. Nessie just laughed and said "Wait till you've nane!" An a was just trying tae get a bit of expert advice here on the state of things tae come, no offence Maud, just thought you could give me the benefit of your years. You never know what's ahead of ya, but ... No baldy fanny for me, my man loves a hairy Mary, no offence, Audra.

Audra *is beside herself with shock.* **Maud** *looks really embarrassed and is regretting bringing her posh friend to the sauna.*

Pearl *starts to do her toes, inadvertently flashing at **Maud** and **Audra** who leave looking shocked and disgusted.*

| Gertie | *(Moves to **Audra's** seat and informs **Pearl** on what has been staring **Audra** in the face:)* Christ's sake Pearl, the first time she comes to the sauna and you're showing your all tae her, nae wonder the lassie left, probably never come   here again. |

Pearl is embarrassed. They are surprised when **Audra** and **Maud** return.

| Gertie | Oh, she's back - must have liked what she saw, you're in there, Pearl! |

| Maud | I hear they are changing the toilets in the town centre. |

Pearl puts more water on the coals. The scene closes in a flurry of steam. **All** exit.

Scene 3: On Becoming A Woman

The women sit in a semi-circle and have a natural conversation on the topic.

Joan   What do you remember about becoming a woman?

Lorraine   Emotions and tears.

Irene   Crying into my candlewick bedspread.

Joyce   Starting my period! I was only nine!

Lorraine   Period pains.

Joan   Dr White's hammocks.

Irene   Running out of STs and having to use rags.

Joan   Boobs at twelve.

Joyce   I felt like a woman when my breasts got fondled for the first time.

Lorraine   I must, I must increase my bust.

A young woman with smaller breasts steps forward.

Mammalogue - *written by Emma Boulton Roe*

I waited twelve years for these ... *(points at breasts:)* I grew up hoping that a distant relative with massive breasts would arrive at the door - "Ta da! I pass on this heaving bosom to you, my dear." Unfortunately, all the women in my family are breastically challenged. The only large body parts passed on by our women are chunky calves and sizable ears!

Practically speaking, small breasts are great. You can lie on your front, run for the bus, buy your tops at Tammy Girl ... but not so great when you're trying to buy regular-sized clothes that tend to have boob shapes built in. That saggy-top look isn't so great! Anyway ...

Having reached 18 and never growing past a B cup, I had resigned myself to a life of Wonder Bras and clever dressing to create the illusion of curves up top. For years I felt like my top and bottom halves didn't match. The inherited chunky calves came free along with a pair of muscly thighs and a slightly rounded tummy ... And then there's my top half - scrawny, chest like a xylophone, visible collar bones, tiny tits ... I felt like one of those children's books where you can mix and match different characters. Arnie on the bottom half, Kate Moss up top!

So I did what any neurotic woman with a body issue would do. I tried to get rid of my curves. I dieted, exercised, invested in those magic pants that suck everything in ... But your shape is your shape. I eventually gave up and tried to love me the way I am. Not an easy task in this day and age, with supermodels on every glossy mag and super waifs on every screen!

Then one day, after another pregnancy scare with an asshole of a boyfriend - now an ex, I'm pleased to say! - I took a visit to my local family planning clinic. A very nice doctor went through all my options and humouring my request for a miracle pill (that would make me skinny, make my periods regular, light and pain-free, wouldn't turn me into a hormonal crying psychopath and would finally make my boobs grow at least one cup-size bigger) he prescribed me with a mini pill. He did suggest that no such pill existed and that perhaps my contraceptive needs should be the most important bit ...

Well, that shows him up! I didn't put on weight, I'm not nuts (at least by Corby standards!) and I grew two whole cup sizes! Yay! Now at the ripe old age of twenty-four I finally have a bosom and curves that I love all over! All I need now is a miracle pill that allows you to eat an entire cake factory without a hint of cellulite ... I'm sure they're working on it! *(She returns to the circle.)*

Scene 4: Contraception

MUSIC: RADIO CONDOM ADVERT

Joan   Once we have women's bodies, we have he risk of falling pregnant. Here is an extract from "Tackling Teenage Pregnancy", a documentary drama written from Corby stories. At this point in the play, Cath and Lisa are 15 and having to make decisions about contraception.

Cath and Lisa are two 15-year-old friends trying to make sensible contraceptive choices. Lisa is sitting on a table swinging her legs. Cath joins her. Both are in school uniform.

Cath   Hi Lisa, guess where I've been?

Lisa   Where?

Cath   To the doctor's.

Lisa   Are you ill then?

Cath   No. Do I look ill? *(Waiting for more questions. Lisa does not respond. Excitedly:)* I'm on the pill!

Lisa   *(Sarcastically:)* Oh great, why do you need that?

Cath	I thought you'd be pleased. When Lee and I were babysitting the other night, we got bit carried away and nearly did it. So, then I gave him a handie and he shot his load all over me! What a mess! And I thought I might get pregnant like Carrie, you know, without him bein' inside me, so I went …
Lisa	Shut up!
Cath	You're in a mood. Anyway, I went to my doctor's. I was too shy to tell him I wanted it just in case - so I lied about my periods. I think he guessed, anyway - he made me feel really special and grown-up and I saw the practice nurse who was dead easy to talk to, and I asked her everything I wanted to know, like would it hurt?
Lisa	Will you shut up!
Cath	Lisa, what's the matter?
Lisa	Remember club XS - I did it - with Kev!
Cath	Eeugh! He's gross - how could you do it to Kayleigh? What was it like?
Lisa	I feel awful - I was pilled up - out of it - he said he'd take me home but then we were in the back of his car …

Cath	*(Self-centeredly:)* Lee and I are going to do it somewhere really special for our first time.
Lisa	Well, then I didn't come on yesterday, so I thought I might be pregnant and went for a pregnancy test at the Women's Centre.
Cath	It would be too soon to tell.
Lisa	I know that now! Anyway, she made me an appointment with a doctor I didn't know - so my Mum wouldn't find out, and he gave me the morning-after pill.
Cath	*(Cocky:)* You mean emergency contraception.
Lisa	Yeah, yeah.
Cath	*(Calculating:)* Were you in time?
Lisa	Only just - I've got to remember to take the other tablet tonight.
Cath	*(Clocking it all:)* Is that why you weren't at school this morning? Did he put you on the pill too?

Lisa	No. He didn't have time - he had to dash out. But worse still, I've got to go and get checked out '"'down there" in case I've got something, and it sounds awful.
Cath	That sounds gross!
Lisa	Will you come with me?
Cath	Yeah, of course. Look, my dad will be in for his tea soon, so come round mine with me and we can keep talking.
Lisa	It's over in Kettering at the hospital and I might bump into my mum. Tell you what, I'll come over to Bodywise with you too, then we can get you on the pill. *(They exit, chatting.)*

MUSIC: IS SHE REALLY GOING OUT WITH HIM?
- JOE JACKSON

Joan	One year later, their friend Kayleigh is having a party, having just got engaged to Kev.

MUSIC: CLUB MUSIC

*Enter **Lisa** and **Cath** in party gear.*

Lisa	What's up with you?

Cath	I'm pissed off. Lee and I have been going out with each other for nearly two years and no-one's buying us a drink. And he's only doing that to get in her knickers, like he got in yours.
Lisa	*(Angry at her friend's loose tongue; speaking through gritted teeth)* Look, I told you that in secret, anyway what do you know about sex - you're still a virgin!
Cath	We do stuff - just not that. I'm waiting till I'm 16 - till it's legal.
Lisa	Leave them alone - they're happy - they've just got engaged.
Cath	I'm just worried about her, that's all. He's 19 - shouldn't you warn her about Kev?
Lisa	*(Emphatically:)* NO! *(Turns away.)*
Cath	Would you tell me if you shagged Lee?
Lisa	Cath, how could you say that? Kev and me happened a year ago. I was pilled up - I didn't even like it! It hurt and they're all as bad as each other, anyway I don't see what all the fuss is about - shagging, bonking, screwing around. There's more to life than boys, you know!

Cath	Oh yeah, like what?
Lisa	Parties, clubbing, having a good time, hanging out with your mates oh - and girls. *(**Cath** splutters on her drink in surprise.)* Would you like another drink?

***Both** exit.*

MUSIC: CLUB MUSIC (up loud)

Joan	Six months further down the line, Lisa is working in a café instead of attending school.

**MUSIC: WILL YOU STILL LOVE ME TOMORROW?
- THE SHIRELLES**

***Lisa** enters, puts on pinny and hat and turns on music.
Cath enters behind her and begins to swap the music.*

Lisa	What are you doing?
Cath	*(Crossly, turning the music off:)* Trying to find some decent tunes. This is crap - get some proper music.
Lisa	Well, I like it and so do the customers!
Cath	How's it going?

Lisa	It's great here - I can do what like - and I'm coming in in the week now, don't you dare tell anyone.
Cath	You'll get well wrecked! Is this it then? "D'ya want fries with that, love?" for the rest of your life?
Lisa	Why not? I'm having fun and I'm saving money to get my own place.
Cath	I wish you'd come back to school, it's not the same without you.
Lisa	What's the point? I've only got my English and maths left to do. Anyway, I'll be finished in June and then I'll be in here full-time.
Cath	What about college?
Lisa	What about it? I can always go later and do evening classes. I mean who wants a load of debt around their neck? You've got to pay for your education, you know?
Cath	Well, I miss you.
Lisa	What's up with you?
Cath	I've had two periods this month.
Lisa	Go and see your doctor then.

Cath	And - *(Pointedly:)* I keep being sick.
Lisa	*(Missing the point:)* It's probably something you ate.
Cath	Lee suggested that I get a pregnancy test.
Lisa	What for? You're on the pill!
Cath	Yeah, and I've never missed taking one - and Lee and me have only been having sex for the last few months.
Lisa	Too much information.
Cath	I did get a test. *(Pause.)*
Lisa	And ...? *(Holding still.)*
Cath	It was positive.
Lisa	What happened then? *(**Lisa** freezes where she is.)*

Cath moves to the centre of the stage and speaks directly to the audience.

Cath	We went over to Kettering and brought a cheap test at Savers. Then we went to McDonalds - what a place to find out! First thing we done was look round the shops at how much stuff costs. There's no way we could afford a baby. Lee's only got his apprenticeship and I'm still at school. But you know how anti-abortion we both are. We went for counselling - talked about it for ages. In the end ...*(Dramatic pause while tension builds:)* We decided on a termination. It was really traumatic for both of us. The gynaecologist had no respect for me, he looked at Lee the whole time, he wouldn't speak to me. I had nightmares about him operating on me. They forgot about me after the operation, I was left alone in a room. When Lee finally found me. they'd mixed up my notes. Oh yeah, they assumed I was a slag and gave me a pill for chlamydia too. Lee and I are still together but it doesn't feel the same any more, and I'm falling behind at school. Neither of us could tell our parents.

MUSIC: YOU DON'T HAVE TO SAY YOU LOVE ME - DUSTY SPRINGFIELD

*Exit **Cath** and **Lisa**.*

Scene 5: Pregnancy Memories

The women sit in the semicircle and talk together.

Joan
Of course, finding out you are pregnant when it is planned is a different matter altogether.

Joyce
I remember knowing when I conceived on both occasions.

Irene
I found out I was pregnant the day JFK got shot. I came home full of news and found everyone watching TV. No-one wanted to know. I cried buckets.

Joan
I remember in 1979 they were selling houses cheap and my husband had his redundancy money, so we were looking at a house on Shetland Way. I told him that it was only a three-bedroomed house and there were seven of us. Not six! That's when I announced that pregnancy.

Leslie
I wanted to shout it from the rooftops, but it was Easter so the surgery couldn't confirm it till after the break. I knew inside I was, though.

Lola
And being pregnant - what a palaver!

Irene
Putting on my tights.

Joan	Trying to get up.
Betty	I was chuffed to bits at my new size-38 breasts, and then they went as soon as I gave birth!
Barbara	Being in agony in a butcher's queue.

This section can continue as each new performer adds her own stories.

Joan	Sadly, for all too many women, however, pregnancy is a time of pain and torment at the hands of abusive partners.

One of the women steps forward and reads:

She Washed the Floor - *written by Anna Swir*

He came back after midnight
And collapsed in the doorway.
She heaved him into the house.

He tumbled into bed with his boots on, vomiting
He made a grab for her, she wouldn't have it
He punched her in the stomach, and started to snore.

She washed the floor, changed the cover on the eiderdown,
And knocked on her neighbours' door.
She's about to give birth.

She returns to the semicircle for the next round of memories.

Scene 6: Birth Memories

Betty   I remember when I was about to give birth for the first time I went into labour prematurely and phoned Dr Carroll to come out. He needed to give me an internal so he said "Bottoms up", and me, new to all this, I climbed up on the bed on all fours. I was wondering what he was going to do.
He just said "Never mind, Elizabeth."

Barbara   What happened next?

Betty   I could go on.

Leslie   I was with my daughter during her first birth and I went into sympathetic labour. I'm keeping well away this time.

Lola   My mum had that sort of connection with me too. She was awake all night when I was in labour.

Joan   I remember the bitch of a midwife. And at the end of it all I needed 38 stitches!

Lola   Where did they find room for all of those?

Joan   Inside and out!

All cross their legs and cringe.

Lorraine	Makes me glad I never had any kids!
Joyce	I had so many stitches the midwife commented on the pattern!
Lola	And then after all that pain and agony, they write "normal delivery" on your notes.
Barbara	Well, I was 17 when I had my first, and I knew nothing.

MUSIC: CHILDBIRTH SONG – SANDRA KERR

Alice's Secret - *written by Irene Hamilton*

Joan   Of course there is less stigma about girls having their babies young nowadays. It wasn't always accepted, and women often had no choice.

Alice, a woman in her fifties, walks slowly and painfully
onto the set. She sits very slowly on the chair. Takes time to settle herself, grimacing as she does so. Sighs painfully, and then notices the audience and proceeds to tell them her story.

Alice My name is Alice ... Ooh! I ache ... It hurts me so much. *(Holds one of her hips. Sighs again and changes position to the other hip:)*
I miss him so much ... I wasn't born here ... I'm an exile from my homeland ...Corby is where I live ... *(Changes position once more to the other hip. Looks once more around her, and looks at the audience as if deciding whether to go on. Then sighs once more.)*

When I was fourteen, I was baby-sitting for one of my father's friends when he came back early and alone. He had left his wife behind. *(Changes position once more.)*

He raped me! When he had done with me, he pushed me outside and I never went back there again ... I was so numb for a long time ... I never told anybody, but later when I started to swell up, mum noticed that I was getting bigger. She told my dad and he called me all the filthy bitch names he could think of - "Slut!Whore! ... No daughter of mine ... " Never asked how it happened ... couldn't have told him how it got there ... I didn't know about babies in those days ... I hadn't a clue until years later how babies came to be in there.

*(**Alice** changes again painfully to the other hip:)* They were so ashamed of me ... didn't want the neighbours to know. Sent me to live with my Aunt Betty in the country. I was kept out of sight ... Whenever anyone came to the door, I had to hide ... Never left the house for months ... Then I was sent to one of those homes for unmarried mothers for the last week before ... *(Silence.)*

The birth was terrifying ... I was made to feel like a criminal ... I was split from stem to stern ... *(Alice begins to play with the buttonhole at the hem of her jumper:)* I named him Stephen ...

He was taken off immediately he came out ... I never saw him again ...

(Drops her eyes to the floor and an even longer silence ensues. Finally, she changes to the other hip and looks up. There are tears in her eyes.)

They sent me home after about a week, without my baby ... It was my sister's birthday ... they were having a party. Nobody mentioned the baby. Nobody asked what I had ... It was just as if it had never happened... I was only fifteen! Forget, do you? *(Looks up at the audience:)* I think of him every single day now. I miss him so much ... I wish I could hold him just once ... They never let me ... How could they?

(Her voice begins to break as she tells the next part:) He would be 41 tomorrow ... *(Wraps her arms around herself and rocks gently back and forth)* ... You never ...

I left home and came to live in Corby when I was eighteen. What a lovely time I had after that. I found a workmate to live with. We had a flat together and we were out every weekend, dancing, pictures in Kettering. What a lot of fun we had. It was so great just to be free!

I met a lovely boy. He was so good to me. We got married and we had three girls. Lovely girls ... He treated me like a queen … I never told them about Stephen … But I never forgot him … My husband died last month and I ache for him … I wish he was here to hold me tomorrow. I miss them … It hurts … It hurts sooo much … I ache, ooh! I ache so much …

There was no option for girls like me but to have our babies adopted. Maybe that's why so many of today's young girls decide to keep their babies. Maybe it was just Madonna's song "Papa don't preach, I'm in trouble" that helped to change things for them. I don't know at all - but I had no Madonna - I was just a BAD GIRL!

(**Alice** *changes position once more, hugs herself and retreats into her pain:*)

Even now for those young women who have their babies, life is not exactly a bed of roses. (*She exits slowly.*)

MUSIC: PAPA DON'T PREACH - MADONNA

The Birth

SET: A waist-high table centre stage which acts as the operating table. Two small stools which act as stirrups during the examination.

PROPS: Trolley offstage loaded with a metal roasting tin containing a sink plunger, metal salad tongs, a doll, a large white sheet, a white blood-stained cloth, two sets of scrubs and operating theatre masks, one pair of Marigold gloves and a back-opening hospital gown.

*The scene begins with pregnant 16-year-old **Kayleigh** in an obvious state of panic, looking down at her groin as her waters break, exclaiming ad lib that she has wet herself.*

*The **Midwife,** in blue scrubs, enters brusquely, talking to **Kayleigh** reassuringly as she leads her to the table.*

*The **Consultant**, in green scrubs, enters carrying a clipboard.*

Consultant	Kayleigh Wilson, 16. God, doesn't she realise the probability of a caesarean, low birth weight, 60% chance of infant mortality? Why can't they wait? She should still be playing with Barbie dolls! *(Glancing briefly at **Kayleigh**:)* Hello Kayleigh. *(To **Midwife**:)* Labour?
Midwife	Twelve hours.
Consultant	Contractions?

Midwife	Two minutes.
Consultant	Pain relief?
Midwife	Epidural, due to take effect.
Consultant	Baby?
Midwife	Heart monitored.
Consultant	Dilation?
Midwife	Vaginal examination due.
Consultant	Very well, I will perform a vaginal examination.

*They reposition **Kayleigh** on her back with knees open for an internal examination. The **consultant** ostentatiously puts on Marigold gloves and peers inside.*

Consultant	That's right love, get your legs open. Hmmm. Yes, yes, she's fully dilated now, but the baby's head is not descending, so I'm afraid it'll have to be assisted delivery. Get the trolley.

Midwife exits and returns with the delivery trolley and a stool which she places by the table. The Consultant has put the stools up on the table to create stirrups and Kayleigh now lies with her calves placed on the stools. Consultant improvises telling Kayleigh what he is doing and checking an imaginary heart monitor screen. He also reassures her that the epidural will take effect any time soon.

MUSIC: LOUD GYM MUSIC (with thumping heartbeat)

Consultant   *(To Midwife:)* Forceps, please.

Midwife hands over the tongs which the Consultant brandishes in the air before miming using them to deliver the baby. In time to the beat of the music the two medics repeat the following instructions a few times.

Consultant   Here we go. Just like in ante-natal classes, and push!

Midwife   Breathe!

Consultant   Push!

Midwife   Breathe!

Consultant   No good! Ventouse!

They swop the salad tongs for the sink plunger and repeat the push/breathe sequence a few times.

Consultant *(Impatiently:)* Oh, you can do better than that for Christ's sake, it's only a baby! Now push. *(Suddenly leaping into action:)* Foetal distress, emergency caesarean, get the consent form.

They mime getting a consent form signed, take the stools down, sit her up and help her into the hospital gown, lie her down again, twizzle body.

Consultant Let's get you down to theatre.

> *They both put on theatre caps and masks and then hold the sheet up together to disguise the "operation". They mime handing the scalpel over and then the **Midwife** holds the sheet whilst the **Consultant** pretends to operate and gets the doll from behind the sheet. As the "baby" emerges, the **Consultant** places it on **Kayleigh,** who does not respond. **Consultant** hands baby to **Midwife** and takes sheet with one hand whilst miming sewing up with the other. The **Midwife** goes to one side and swaddles the baby before handing it gently to **Kayleigh**. The medics then carry on mopping up **Kayleigh** using the blood-stained sheet. Putting everything back in the tray, they sit **Kayleigh** up and twizzle her round to face the audience, pat her on the back and exit, already discussing the next delivery.*

> *As they exit, the music stops.*

Scene 7: Motherhood

Kayleigh

That's when it hit me, I had a daughter - my daughter. When they first showed me Jasmine, I was so out of it, all I could think about was sleeping. I watched her sleeping in my arms, the most beautiful baby I'd ever seen, perfect.

I never knew there could be love like this in the world. Having her hurt, but! Really hurt! Like all my insides were being ripped apart. I'm glad I had the epidural. When I got to theatre, I was kinda numb; but I could still feel them poking around - weird!

The midwife was really nice, but I wanted Sally - the one from Sure Start, she's more like a friend, I didn't like the consultant guy - I suppose it's 'cos I'm young - but he kept talking down to me, all these big words I didn't understand. And the things they used on me! Well scary! The midwife came to see me after, and explained things to me, but I'm still confused. Anyway, she's here now - six pounds two ounces, not bad.

How am I coping? I know I look after her, I don't care what anyone says: it depends on the person not the age. I do love her but now I realise how different my life would have been - freer, easier, if I didn't have her. I haven't had time to think about college, I went for an audition the other week - I got the part - but I can't get a babysitter, I can't afford the bus and I'm always tired.

I thought Kev would help like he said he would, but that didn't last and neither did we, and the last time he had her she came back with really bad nappy rash. Well, he's not taking her this time, is he, Jasmine? No.

She exits with the baby.

MUSIC: CELINE DION - BABY CLOSE YOUR EYES - and baby crying

This scene is mimed to the following anonymous poem which can be either read live by another performer or be pre-recorded.

*Enter **New Mother** carrying swaddled baby. She is clearly exhausted. She lays the sleeping baby in the crib and as she steps away the baby begins to cry. She has clearly had enough and tries unsuccessfully to settle the child. Once her own **Mother** - now a gran – arrives, she curls up and goes to sleep herself whilst her **Mother** takes over.*

I have borne a life

It came screaming from my insides and, like an Aztec deity, Demands the sacrifice of my life.

I bend over the small doll and we look into each other's eyes.

You won't get the better of me, I say
I won't be the shell of the egg you crack open as you burst into the world
Nor the footbridge you cross to get to your own life. I'll defend myself.

I bend over the small doll and notice a tiny movement in a tiny finger
Which no time ago was inside me
Under whose delicate skin flows my own blood.
And that's it - I'm submerged by a towering bright wave of humility.

Helpless, I drown.
Is it myself I worship in the fruit of my own body?
Am I sacrificing myself to the cannibal god of instinct?
Where will I summon the strength to resist her, weak as she is?

The small doll needs me as much as she needs air.
I submit willingly to being swallowed by love
I submit to being swallowed like air by her tiny greedy lungs of life.

*Enter **Narrator** who reads the bulk of the piece whilst **Irene** and **Barbara** speak odd lines. **Irene** acts out the story of the poem.*

Narrator   The old woman danced in her kitchen.

*Irene rushes on stage excitedly, dances, then decides to go.
She clears up the kitchen and keeps singing:*

Irene	I'm a Gran, I'm a Gran, I'm a Gran!
Narrator	Her shoes fell off and her toes were bare. She flung her apron into the air. And all the pins fell out of her hair.
Irene	I'm a Gran, I'm a Gran, I'm a Gran!
Narrator	The old woman sang in her kitchen.
Irene	I'm a Gran, I'm a Gran, I'm a Gran!
Narrator	Her voice was cracked and out of tune But her heart was high as a runaway balloon. And the winter sun shone down like June
Irene	I'm a Gran, I'm a Gran, I'm a Gran!

*Enter **Barbara**.*

Narrator	The neighbour came into her kitchen. She said:
Barbara	You may be a Gran but you look just like a demented hen. It's quite disgraceful, especially when You're over three-score years and ten!

Irene glances at **Barbara**, *walks past, gets her case.*

Irene   Push off.

Narrator   She said -

Irene   I'm a Gran!

Exit **Barbara**. **Irene** *mimes sitting on a train, watching out of the window. She eventually arrives at her daughter's house, rushes in and picks up the baby.*

Narrator   On the train the wheels were repeating
                       You're a Gran, you're a Gran, you're a
                       Gran!
                       It seemed like a lifetime rolling past
                       But breathless she reached her goal at
                       last.
                       And whispered as she held him fast

Irene   I'm your Gran, I'm your Gran, I'm your
                       Gran!

MUSIC: SEVEN SECONDS - NENEH CHERRY

ACT TWO

Scene 1: Food Lovers' Group

SET: A semi-circle of chairs, a small desk and chair, a flipchart and a weighing scales.

MUSIC: PERFECT 10 – THE BEAUTIFUL SOUTH

Enter various women attending the equivalent of a Slimming World session but for people trying to eat more, not less. They improvise greetings and chat, take it in turns to step on the scales and get weighed in before rejoining the group.

MUSIC FADES

Leslie	*(To **Irene**:)* Ooh, I'm busting for the loo!
Irene	*(Carrying a cardy:)* Here, I'll hold your things.
Leslie	No, I'll wait until I've been weighed. Can I borrow your cardy? I haven't even got a jacket.

Leslie struggles quickly into Irene's cardy which is too big. She goes over to the group leader Joyce, who is weighing them in.

Joyce	Next. Get on the scales, they never lie. *(**Leslie** gets on.)* What have you been doing? You've lost two pounds. I'm

117

	sorry, you'll have to do better than that! Your clothes are hanging off you!
Leslie	But I'm finding it hard to eat - I'm just not hungry!
Joyce	Well, buy our Cordon Bleu cookbook. *(Shows her:)* Every recipe uses only the best ingredients, full flavour, full fat. Plenty to tempt your taste buds. Next!
Irene	*hands over card and gets on scales.*
Joyce	Well done, that's three pounds on! What's your secret?
Iren	Chocolate pudding and a special Burns Night feast of haggis, neeps and tatties.

Joyce writes up summary of weights whilst women chat, then announces the results.

Joyce	I'm pleased to tell you that everybody, bar Leslie *(glaring at **Leslie**:)* - who I will talk to later *(handing her a Barbie doll)* - has put on weight. Especially Irene who gets this week's Venus award. *(Hands a chubby cherub to **Irene**.)*

All applaud.

Joyce	OK ladies, who's done their homework? Let's hear some menus to make your mouths water!

Whole group read out examples of their dream meal, with as much delight and mouth-watering relish as they can. **Leslie** *says nothing.*

Joyce   Come on Leslie, at least try.

Leslie   Well, I love salad!

Joyce   *(Exasperatedly:)* Right ladies, let's help Leslie. We'll do a fattening food list.

The group take turns to call out foods e.g. salad cream, chips, chocolate, crisps.

Joan   Cheese.

Joyce   And how have you been resisting your diets? What about you? *(Looks at* **Betty**.*)*

Betty   Well, I'm not on one. It's my husband. He's on that Weetabix diet, but he's getting awful scrawny. I don't like him without the meat on him. But he keeps trying to get me to diet too.

Joyce   Were you tempted?

Betty   I'm afraid I was. I couldn't resist it. This Sunday I got a big cucumber ... *(Pause.)* Halved it in two ... *(Remembers eating it:)* Ooh! It was lovely!

Joan	*(Sitting next to her, raises eyebrows wondering exactly what she did with the cucumber:)* The mind boggles. No wonder you've lost weight.
Betty	*(Not getting the innuendo, and feeling guilty about her slimming sin:)* I took the skin off as well!
Gertie	*(Well up with the innuendo:)* You'd have been safer leaving it shrink-wrapped!

Irene splutters her whisky.

Gertie	Well, I was on Rosemary Conlon's fat-free diet and the other day at the supermarket, I got to the checkout before I realised I had a trolley full of no-fat yoghurt!
Joan	What did you do?
Gertie	Put the lot back!
Joyce	Well done.
Barbara	I was with Weight Watchers and I still find myself counting points.
Joan	Me too. I found some no-sugar, low-fat, low-calorie crispbread with no points!
Lola	What's the point in no points?

Charlotte	I was on the grapefruit diet and I couldn't resist this week. I put sugar on.
Irene	The smell of my farts on the cabbage soup diet put me off more than anything …
Joyce	*(Losing the focus of the group, claps loudly:)* OK, ladies, what about cravings?
Gertie	I've been gagging for a Slimfast.
Barbara	Cabbage soup.
Charlotte	Beetroot.
Joa	Celery.
Irene	Rice cake and Ryvitas.
Joan	*(To **Betty**:)* You'll have been craving cucumber.
Betty	I love cucumber.
Leslie	I love carrots.
Joyce	Let me share our thought for the week.

She turns flipchart paper to reveal in large lettering the words "NO GOING BACK".

Joyce	And to finish tonight, who is our fave babe this week?

She turns flipchart paper to reveal -

All	Dawn French!
Joyce	And we'll dedicate our closing prayer this week, to -

She turns flipchart paper to reveal -

All	Victoria Beckham!
Joyce	And now our closing prayer - please stand. It's on your card if you are new.
All	*(Standing to recite:)* We thank our higher power for the gift of food he brings We promise we will honour him and eat our favourite things We love ourselves for who we are, the food we eat is yummy Our shape's our own, we love our curves, our hips and bums and tummies
Joyce	Anyone for Tai Chi?

The women move chairs to create a gym and then either do Tai Chi or gym exercises.

MUSIC: PUMP IT UP - ELVIS COSTELLO

Scene 2: Cosmetic Surgery

Selina, *the gym tutor, steps forward.*

Selina   I'm Selina and slim, never on the gin
                      In fact, I teach a class for reduction of
                      the arse
                      They worship my body so lithe and thin
                      I ignore remarks about breasts. Some
                      are a bit dim
                      I make lists and register all their eating
                      habits
                      Sometimes it makes me vomit
                      When I see they eat like rabbits
                      For when the class is finished, I rush
                      home to my mum
                      Where she fixes up a meal to put
                      calories on my bum.
                      But upstairs to the privy - no-one ever
                      knows.
                      Two fingers down my throat, flush
                      And the contents are disposed.

*Enter **Tiffany,** a thirty-five-year-old model.*

Tiffany   *(To **Selina**:)* There are other ways to
                      keep your figure, you know. *(Hands out
                      leaflets, saying to group and audience:)*
                      Hi! I'm Tiffany, I'm doing a talk about
                      cosmetic surgery.

Faces audience to deliver her talk - taken from Eve Ensler's play "The Good Body".

I've heard people say that they've been changed by someone, but they don't mean literally. My surgeon literally changed me with his hands, with his instruments, with his vision. He removed some things and added others. I'm not anything like the person I was six years ago.

I went to him originally because another doctor had really botched my breast implants. My left breast was deflated and looked really odd, like all the life from it was gone. Ham, that's my surgeon's name, well, because he looks like one - bald, fat, short - Ham. He was horrified at the mess the previous doctor had made, and he actually seemed a little tiffed with me. Like I wasn't committed to make this the bestest, goodest body it could be. This is Ham's mission. I mean, that's what he does.

I'm not sure that I ever had the confidence to even imagine being perfect. I mean, I liked having a few extra glasses of wine, or sleeping till noon, or letting my hair go unwashed a few extra days.

Ham really changed all that. He's very strict. After I woke up from my first surgery, he was there standing over me. He was very excited. He had taken a life-size photograph of my entire body naked. It felt a bit invasive. I mean, I'm shy and didn't really know him. There were corrective red marks all over my body like the kind you got on your spelling mistakes in seventh grade. I was still groggy, but Ham's enthusiasm got through. "Your body is a map", he said. "These red marks are designated beauty capitals that need renovation and work." That was six years ago and today I am a Ham creation. I've had lipo on my stomach, butt, and thighs. He's gone back in with each at least three times to get it right - well, four, he did my thighs again today. I have newer soya breast implants that do not harden and feel kinder to the touch. That was for Ham.

We started dating after he made my tits softer. That really turned him on. He was doing the check-up exam about a month after the surgery. He was feeling my breasts, all doctorly. Then something changed. It just got different. Before I knew it, Ham had climbed on top of the examining table and we were doing it. I think how wonderful it must be for him to actually make love to what he's created. It must be very satisfying, and it's good. Twice during sex he's discovered areas with his fingers and tongue that needed more work.

Ham says it's good I'm only thirty-five, so all this will last for a while. It was after he did my lips that he proposed to me. I think it was my little pouty pouch that made me irresistible. We're married now, two years. Some people have cafés or bookshops - we've got my body. It's our small business. It's a joke Ham and I make, but we're doing pretty well. I've won several major beauty contests and I've booked lots of commercials and magazines. But more importantly, my body is a great advertisement for Ham. He's gotten so much new business.

Ham is devoted to me. He is always so kind, particularly when I first wake up from surgery. He knows how much it terrifies me. Ever since the "cardiac episode." It was during my second breast implant that my heart kind of stopped. I felt so bad for Ham. He had just finished this beautiful work on my breasts and he was going to have to ruin it by compressing my chest. Fortunately, he waited and my heart started on its own.

Sometimes I worry what will happen when he runs out of parts of me to change. Or that he'll be intimidated by the perfection of his own creation. But what worries me most is that he'll just get finished and lose interest. That's why I've secretly never given up ice-cream.

Joan	It's got to beat all this effort.
Irene	There's more to it than you think! What about all the pain and risk of it going wrong?
Joan	No pain, no gain!
Lola	I know women whose boyfriends have bought them cosmetic surgery as a Xmas present. Imagine having your breasts sliced up for Xmas!
Lorraine	I know a woman whose boyfriend did that but she left him so he never got any pleasure!
Joyce	I know a woman who had it done for medical reasons and it completely transformed her life. She was five feet ten and a 56-inch bust and the confidence after her breast reduction was amazing.

Barbara   Medical reasons I can accept, but my neighbour's daughter had a boob job done even though her mum had breast cancer.

Leslie   I nursed a woman this week after a boob job. *(Pause.)* A double mastectomy.

Scene 3: Breasts

Irene   This poem is for those who never lived
              to tell their tale.

*Others place chairs in a row along the front, saying the
name of a woman who has died of breast cancer as they
do. Then, as an ensemble, they use physical theatre to
create still tableaux to this poem.*

The Mountains are Moving - *from We'Moon 2005*

The women are coming together - by tens, by hundreds
Out of the hospital beds, off of the X-ray tables
Bald-headed women, one-breasted women

With bodies scarred and carved, pickled with poison to attack
The poison they breathed/they ate/their children sucked.
They are talking, talking, talking their stories

They are holding each other sobbing, they are beating the
drums
They are drumming pounding drumming

They are laughing fiercely to be living.
Living, and fierce, together.
And Mama, the breasted mountains are shaking.

I knew, when you lay broken and moaning
Your chest flattened and stitched - brain, bone, lungs on fire
I knew that someday the flaming women would erupt
Someday they would drum the bedrock into motion
They would fault the poison makers, find each other
With cadence of love and fury.

You would have loved to be among them, Mama.

128

I see you, and an army of your flat-chested ghost sisters
Pounding, pounding on the mantle of the world
The drumskin is tight and thin,
The living women match you beat for beat
No wonder the cliffs are trembling.
I need not tell you, Mama, that the mountains are moving.

MUSIC: MOTHER I FEEL YOU – EARTH, WIND & FIRE

One or several women step forward to read this group of three poems.

Ode to a Mammogram *- Anonymous*

For years and years they told me: Be careful of your breasts
Don't ever squeeze or bruise them, and give them monthly tests

So I heeded all their warnings, and protected them by law
Guarded them very carefully, and I always wore my bra

After 60 years of astute care my gyno, Dr Pruitt
Said I should get a mammogram. "OK," I said, "let's do it."

"Stand up here, real close", she said. She got my boob in line
"Tell me when it hurts," she said, "Ah yes! Right there, that's fine."

She stepped upon a pedal; I could not believe my eyes!
A plastic plate came slamming down, my hooter's in a vice!

My skin was stretched and mangled from underneath my chin
My poor boob was being squashed to Swedish pancake thin,

Excruciating pain I felt, within its vice-like grip,
A prisoner in this vicious thing. My poor defenceless tit!

"Take a deep breath", she said to me - who does she think she's kidding?
My chest is mashed in her machine, and woozy I am getting.

"There, that's good," I heard her say (the room was slowly swaying)
"Now, let's have a go at the other one." Have mercy, I was praying.

It squeezed me from both up and down, it squeezed me from both sides.
I bet SHE'S never had this done, to HER tender little hide.

Next time they make me do this I will request a blindfold
I have no wish to see again my knockers getting steam-rolled.

If I had no problem when I came in, I surely have one now
If there had been a cyst in there it would have gone "ker-pow!"

This machine was created by a man, of this I have no doubt
I'd like to stick his balls in there, and see how THEY come out.

Scene 4: Aging

Warning - *by Jenny Joseph*

When I am an old woman, I shall wear purple
With a red hat which doesn't go, and doesn't suit me
And I shall spend my pension on brandy and summer gloves
And satin sandals, and say we've no money for butter.
I shall sit down on the pavement when I am tired
And gobble up samples in shops and press alarm bells
And run my stick along the public railings
And make up for the sobriety of my youth.
I shall go out in my slippers in the rain
And pick flowers in other people's gardens and learn to spit.
You can wear terrible shirts and grow more fat
And eat three pounds of sausage at a go or only bread and
pickles for a week And hoard pens and pencils and beer mats
and things in boxes
But now we must have clothes that keep us dry
And pay our rent and not swear in the street
And set a good example for the children.
We must have friends to dinner and read the papers.
But maybe I ought to practise a little now?
So people who know me are not too shocked and surprised
When suddenly I am old and start to wear purple.

New Ways - *by Barbara Hawthorn*

Laying foundations for new ways of living
Finding new ways for receiving and giving
Time on my own and time spent with others
Family or friends, colleagues or lovers.

Time used for doing, time just for being
For touching, for healing, for smelling, for seeing.
Time is what matters at this point in life
No longer as daughter or mother or wife.

Time for the me who has slowly emerged
From the embryo creature so often submerged.
Time to expand, to jump and to fly.
To sing and to dance and to laugh and to cry.

To follow the impulse, to act on the feeling
Skins of the onion are peeling, revealing
Perhaps to disclose that still core of the soul
That wisdom and knowledge to make myself whole.

Old Age Sketch

SET: A room in a care home with a typical high-backed arm chair and side table on one side of the stage, and a carer's rest room with two dining-room chairs and a table on the other side of the stage.

PROPS: A tea tray, photo album, magazines, two mugs.

MUSIC: OLD PHOTOGRAPHS SONG - SANDRA KERR

Freda, an elderly resident in a care home, is sitting in a chair with a photo album. Her Carer enters carrying a tea-tray and talking over her shoulder to another carer, Carer 2, who carries on to the carers' rest room.

Carer	I'll be along in a minute, I've only got Freda to do!

She walks to Freda, puts tray down on side table and tries to take the photo album. Freda resists and they move back and forth with it.

Carer	Oh for goodness' sake Freda, don't start today! I've got enough on my plate without you playing up!

Freda does not answer but holds on to her album.

Carer	Suit yourself! I haven't got time for this. *(starts to walk out.)*
Freda	*(Angrily:) (This was written by the actress playing Freda)*

Who are you seeing? What do you see?
Who are you seeing when you're looking at me?
Just a stupid old woman, who's not very wise
Uncertain of habit with far-away eyes
Who seems not to notice the things that you do
And forever is losing a stocking or shoe.

Is that what you're seeing? Is that who you see?
Then open your eyes, for you're not seeing me!
(Opens album:) Now see who I am as I sit here so still.
As I eat at your bidding, and I drink at your will.

I'm a young child of ten with a father and mother
With sisters and brothers who love one another.
I'm a young girl at sixteen with wings on my feet.
Just hoping that someday a sweetheart I'll meet.

I'm a young bride of twenty - my heart gives a leap
Remembering the vows I have promised to keep.
I'm now on to twenty-five - our children grow fast
But they are bound to each other with a love that should last.

At forty my children soon will be gone
But their dad is still with me - to see I don't moan
At fifty, once more children play round our knee
Once again we knew babies, my husband and me.

Dark days come upon me - my husband is dead
I think of the future and I shudder with dread.
My family is busy with bairns of their own
But I think of the past and the love I have known.

I'm an old woman now, and grace and vigour depart
But thousands of memories still live in my heart
Inside it, you see, a girl still dwells
But now and again my tired heart swells.

I think of the joy - and I think of the pain
But I'm living and loving life over again.
So, open your eyes - please open and see
Not a stupid old woman - look closer - SEE ME!

Carer   Thank you for sharing that with me. I'd
                             love to hear some more about your life.
                             Shall I top up your tea?

*She tops up the tea and then goes over to the rest room
for her own break. **Carer 2** is in carers' rest room with a
cuppa, a magazine and her feet up.*

Carer 2   Where've you been?

Carer   I got caught up with Freda - she was
                             showing me her photo album and
                             telling me about her life.

Carer 2   Oh, I can't be doing with it when they
                             start wittering on. It's bad enough
                             cleaning up their piss without having to
                             listen to their boring reminiscences as
                             well.

Carer   Well, I found it fascinating. I reckon we
                             should be given more time to listen.

Carer 2	If they want to give me more money, OK, I suppose I could pretend to be interested.
Carer	Don't you care about them as people? They could be your mum or dad ... even you one day.
Carer 2	Not if I can help it. I'd top myself before I got stuck in a place like this.
Carer	But we make it like this. I'm often too busy to listen and I do forget that they've led full and interesting lives.
Carer 2	Well, it works both ways. What do they think of us? Just another pair of hands to find things for them, wash them, feed them and wipe their arses. I tell you it's like when the kids were babies all over again.
Carer	Except they couldn't talk and had no lives to tell us about.
Carer 2	You're too soft, you. If you're that bothered about it, go and talk to Matron.
Carer	I might just do that.
Carer 2	Well, back to the grindstone. See you later, Florence Nightingale!

Exit **Carer 2.** *The* **Carer** *turns to the audience and delivers the following poem.*

Poetic Thoughts of a Care Assistant - *Anonymous*

Tell me old woman, what do you feel
About those who tend you, some with great skill
Flighty young nurses, with dreams in their eyes
Not at all caring and not very wise
Who, to your eyes, appear to be blind,
To the person you are, to the life you once led,
Seeing only a body, to be cared for and fed.

Please believe me old woman, we really do care
As we wash you, and feed you, and comb out your hair
As we coax and we wheedle, we beg and we plead
As we try to discover and find what you need
As we help you to find that lost stocking or shoe
Believe me, we do notice the things that you do.

We know the sorrow, we feel the pain
Of joys you have known, which won't come again
We know you have led a very full life
We know you were lover, a mother, a wife
The fun and the laughter, which you once shared
With family and friends, people who cared
Days when it seemed the sun always shone,
Too swiftly passing, forever gone.

We really do notice, we do truly care
Recognising that nature is not always fair.
Seeing the dread which lurks in your eye,
To banish that fear we endlessly try.

For we now lead the life which once you had known,
The seeds of our futures are already sown.
You ask us, old woman, what do you see?
And I speak for us all when I say "I see me"!

MUSIC: OLD PHOTOGRAPHS SONG - SANDRA KERR

Exit **Carer**.

Scene 5: Different Eras

MUSIC: COMPILATION OF SONGS FROM VARIOUS ERAS

The women enter from oldest to youngest, and read their verse of the following poem remaining onstage in a line showing how things changed and allowing all the fashions and eras to be seen. Some verses are read by several women together if they are the same age. The three younger women read the last verse.

When I Was 17 - *by the cast*

When I was a girl, it was "Tea for Two"
Foxtrot, waltz and quickstep - the dances we would do
We wore our dresses with ankles on show
Though some wore trousers, they were new, I never had a go
If a boy took a fancy that's all he took
Though if he persisted, we'd find a nook
For a kiss and a cuddle, but he'd stop if I said no
Though a right Jack the lad would always have a go
We waited till we married to do the evil deed
A ring on someone's finger if he had to spread his seed

The world had gone quite crazy when I was 17
The War had left its mark - we were young and fresh and keen
If you loved a man in uniform the choice was yours to make
The dance halls and the wireless, we ate and had our cake
From Sylvester through to skiffle, ballroom dancing to the jive
Romance was in, we had a laugh, so glad to be alive

139

With our petticoats and backcombed hair and radio Caroline
We loved to dance the creep, the jive - we had a cracking time
Perched high on our stilettos, corsets tight around your tum
At our ballroom classes once a week we'd learn how it was done
Buddy Holly was our hero, Tommy Steele just broke your heart
Brenda Lee, Helen Shapiro, even Cilla played her part
The "birds and bees" was not discussed, a shotgun at the ready
The thing to do was find a chap and then you could go steady

We had John, Paul, George and Ringo with their Beatles hair
And what we did with boys was as much as we would dare
It was getting near the era of free love and birth control
We wore our dresses right up here, you'd really feel the cold
At the youth club, or on Saturday, remember Nellie's Bin?
We'd all huddle in a circle and plan our weekly sin

With our eyes on some young fella, we would twist and turn and flirt
But Nellie's steely eye would watch that nobody got hurt
And if a lassie went too far and earned the name of floozie
We'd breathe a sigh it wasn't us, cos we knew well it could be

The pill was in, our bras were off and caftans covered all
We played records on the radiogram - the Stones, Pink Floyd's *The Wall*
On the way to San Francisco, we would smoke a joint or two
With our flowers and our cheesecloth, we were hippies through and through
At the Pit or Nags in fluoro lights with underwear a-glow
We'd do our thing, and have a sing, and just go with the flow

I listened to my music on a bright red radio
Luxembourg all through the night, my favourite radio show
I'd gaze at David Cassidy hung up there on my wall
With my platform shoes and hot pants, I really stood up tall
At the disco on a Saturday I hoped to find a lad
I'd want to be in his gang but I'd never tell my dad
My mate got caught, she went too far and had to leave the school
A tricky line to tread it was, stay safe, and hip and cool

Grungers, Goths or Grebos, Hippies, Townies, Trendies, Chavs
Drinking alcopops and aftershocks, or pints just like the lads
We listen on our iPods, MP3s, CDs, or vinyl
Ibiza hip hop R&B, your music choice is crucial
Showing thongs and hips and bellies, we roam the clubs and score
Condoms in yer purse to stop the germs and so you can be sure
Morning-after pill the fallback if we're too wrecked and forget
We're free to be just what we like - a lady or ladette.

Betty   I still feel 17 inside. Fancy a jive, Irene?

MUSIC: PEGGY SUE - BUDDY HOLLY

Betty and *Irene* jive.

MUSIC: ROCK AROUND THE CLOCK - BILL HALEY

Cast invite audience up to dance.

CURTAIN

Women of Steel
by
Paula Boulton

First performed at the ARC Theatre,
Corby, on 8th March 2007

Synopsis

Women of Steel tells various stories of the way women in Corby were involved at the Steelworks and how their lives and families were affected by the Steel Strike and eventual closures. It is a historically accurate play and gives an insight into the life of Corby women and the community as they dealt with the inevitable changes wrought by the destruction of the Steel industry.

Notes for the Director

This version of *Women of Steel* is the stage play adapted from the outdoor site-specific performance. The set was kept deliberately simple, and was a table and chairs moved between scenes which served to represent a kitchen, a canteen, an office, a campaign stall, a factory - as required. There is a visual script in existence available on the Shout! Theatre website - www.shouttheatre.org - since projections are an integral part of the script. The original songs can also be downloaded and used.

In the event of a staging of the demonstration – you may wish to contact Warwick University archive, as we did, to get hold of the original banners. We were able to call on former Steelworkers to join the demo wearing their t-shirts and Save our Steel hats. Adaptations would need to be made.

Costumes and Props

The women in the factory scenes wore factory bonnets and tabards from one of our local factories. The cleaners wore overalls. The Pied Piper of Wonderland was dressed like the Pied Piper of Hamlyn. Otherwise, people wore normal clothes appropriate to the era.

If a group of young people is used for the Steel Kids section they should be dressed in black trousers and identical black t-shirts with the same white Steel Kids logo. Photos of the original logo are also available on the Shout! Theatre website.

All the music and visuals referred to in the script are available for download and use at www.shouttheatre.org - which also contains film footage of previous performances to illustrate the way the play was originally conceived and performed.

Characters in Order of Appearance

NARRATOR

IRENE, the Storyteller

GWENDA, a Welsh woman new to Corby, 1934

BRIDIE, her Irish friend

ISA, a Glaswegian widow of a Steelworker, 1960

MAUREEN, a Steelworker from Hartlepool, 1970

CISSIE
ELSIE
MARY   } Cleaners in the Quantivac, 1960
MEGAN

SALLY, a new Cleaner

MAVIS, the supervisor

JO, a young Canteen Worker, 1974

ELAINE
ANNIE
RUBY
JEAN   } Canteen Workers, 1979
YVONNE
ISOBEL

KAREN, Union representative from ISTC
        (Iron and Steel Trades Confederation)

MAUREEN JOHNSON, secretary of ROSAC
        (Retention of Steelmaking at Corby)

PETER
MONTY } Steelworkers from the Save our Steel March

CROWD - supporters, demonstrators and March organisers

MAGGIE THATCHER
BODYGUARDS 1 and 2

PIED PIPER OF WONDERWORLD

JAN
KAREN
JEAN
ANNIE } Box Factory Workers, 1984
JOSIE
YVONNE
ISOBEL

SUPERVISOR at the Box Factory

ELLEN, the Union representative

SUSAN
MARGARET
BETTY
LIZZIE
JOY } Workers at Corby Clothing Company,
JEAN
IRENE
EVELYN

EMMA
JO } Workers at Chocolate Factory in Corby,
JEN

Group of TEENAGERS to perform *Steel Kids*

ACT ONE

Scene 1: Intro

SCREEN: Images of old Corby Village

SET: A table laid as if inside a 1930s house

MUSIC: VILLAGE LIFE

LYRICS:
Village life is a pleasure
Below us the land, above us the sky
Cookie's Corner, that's Mr Cook's
And the paper shop, now that's Mr. Patters'
And Nellie Smith will sell you the gobstoppers
Don't ever say there's nothing to buy
Sarrington's, Hargreaves and Lee's and the Co-op
It's only a village but everyone tries
It's a small place, yet you can say that
Whatever we want, they'll try to supply.

Work there is in Kettering
Or there's the factory in Cottingham
But it's the Ironworks brings most of the money
A shortage of jobs was never the cry
Some will go ploughing and hoeing and sowing
They're out in all weathers, the wet and the dry
But the Ironworks are what matter
Without it the village surely would die.

Everyone knows everyone else
That's from Mr Payne who lives in the big house
To those of us who work in the Works
Be you ever so low, or ever so high
Meet at the church or the scouts or the hall
And with newcomers coming we'll all have to try
To be welcoming and whatever
We think, we'll do our best to hide.

As song ends **Narrator** enters.

Narrator
Rural England in the 1930s. In the county of
Northamptonshire was a small village with an Ironworks
providing its main employment. Stewart and Lloyds
decided to build a Steelworks to exploit the rich seam of
iron ore. But where would the workers come from? And so
began the first wave of immigration to Corby.

Thousands of men from all over, looking for work … and
shortly afterwards, their families.

We want to tell you the story of some of those people, how
the town rose and fell with the Steelworks, and 25 years
since steel, we look at now and the future.

Exit **Narrator**.

MUSIC: JOBS MAY COME

Scene 2: Roots

SCREEN: **SCREEN:** Visual script of the women and where they came from. Their faces appear on screen as they are introduced

Irene, an Aberdonian, enters as Storyteller.

Irene   Hello. I'm Irene. I want to talk to you about where we Women of Steel came from. I know the story goes that Corby was peopled by Glaswegians, but my dad was from Aberdeen, one of many fish workers who moved their families down to Corby in the 50s and 60s. There was a noticeable Aberdonian community with our own meeting place, customs and language. We soon fitted in, and, over time, like with any incoming community, we lost some of our distinctiveness.

Mind you, I well remember taking my two bairns back home for the first time. The look on their faces when they heard me talking to the taxi driver in the dialect of my childhood! It sounded like a foreign language to them.

People came to Corby from all over. A real Heinz 57 varieties. Everyone of them in search of a job and a decent house, yet each with their own unique story.

Betty came from Perth in 1956 when her railwayman father got a job in the works. The family of five lived in a caravan in Burton Latimer at first. A bit of a squeeze when all's said and done. But they settled into their own house in Corby within a year.

A house of your own was one of Corby's biggest attractions. Far better than living in a tenement with four families to a bathroom or having to live with your parents when you got married.

Josie and her family hailed from Ireland. She grew up in Sussex, spent early married life as an army wife in Germany and then settled in Corby in 1969.

Then there's Bridie. She visited her brother in Corby in 1960 on the way back to Ireland from New York. She found him settled in a town with a future. The rest of the family followed shortly afterwards. Corby was a place hard-working people moved to. Often from communities with no prospects.

There was a growing Irish community, which tended to supply the labourers who worked to build the town as it grew. In the sixties, the Catholics held Mass in St. Brendan's school, a sure way to meet others and keep your culture alive. Eventually they built both a clubhouse and a church. This pattern was repeated by most of the incoming communities whatever the religion. As you can see from the number of both clubs and churches across Corby.

Margaret arrived from Aberbargoed in the Welsh Valleys in 1960. Her dad had come here for the Steelworks along with a good few other Welsh miners. He was one of the original Bevin boys, conscripted to the mines during World War II. He was honest about the work he'd done before, whereas some of his mates made out that they had the necessary skills. Guess who got the better jobs?

He already had coal dust in his lungs. Industrial diseases plagued those working in the Works. Many men were left permanently suffering, or succumbed to early death.

And finally Lorraine who was born here in Corby. Polish father. Anglo-Italian mother. A lot of Poles, Latvians, Lithuanians were caught in the crossfire of World War II, and ended up here as Displaced Persons. And of course there were Italian prisoners of war and American servicemen, all adding to the ethnic mix that gives Corby its vibrancy.

Scene 3: Homesick

MUSIC: WELSH MALE VOICE CHOIR

SCREEN: Aberbargoed or Coal Miners

Gwenda, a Welsh woman, enters with a box of cutlery, sits at the table and starts cleaning it. Listening to the music makes her homesick. Bridie, her Irish friend, enters. Gwenda turns off radio.

Bridie	What's up, Gwenda?
Gwenda	Homesick.
Bridie	You'll soon get used to it. Just think about having a house, and a job, and a future for your family.
Gwenda	That's your head talking, and it's my heart that's hurting.
Bridie	Tell me then.
Gwenda	Well, I miss my mum and my sisters for a start. They stayed in Swansea and at least they have each other. And the sea, and things to do. And I miss hearing Welsh and speaking Welsh. Don't you miss home?
Bridie	Sure I do. We all do. (Silence.) I know it seems like a sacrifice now, but just think of your children.

Gwenda	I am doing. Every time I open a drawer or a box of sweets, I find these little notes from Carol saying she wants to go home. She misses her friends and hates it at her new school.
Bridie	There's not much for them to do here, that's true. And when they do play out, they come in filthy dirty, covered in dust. I can never get my washing clean here. God knows what's in the air!
Gwenda	I know there is iron. My Robert was collecting iron filings off the wall. I suppose they'll enjoy the fair though.
Bridie	As long as he remembers to leave the free tickets out.
Gwenda	Is Eamonn on nights?
Bridie	Why do you think I've come round to you? It's like a bleeding morgue round there. Creeping around so as not to wake him. I even hung a blanket up at the window 'cos he says the light keeps him awake.
	I dread the kids coming home from school.
	They need to let off a bit of steam but I'm telling them to shush the whole time. And you know I'm up really early so I

can sort his feet out before he goes to bed. Those clogs may keep their feet safe but they chafe his heels raw.

Gwenda I worry about my Tom's hearing. You know he forgets he's at home and shouts at me as if I'm deaf. He doesn't even realize he's doing it. And Mr Mitchell next door is the same - I can hear every word he says to Jean. And the rest!

Bridie Is it still bad?

Gwenda Mostly at the weekend when he's had a drink.

Bridie It's the kids I feel sorry for.
I remember my dad doing the same to my mum when I was little. I used to huddle under the bedclothes with my eyes tight shut, willing him to stop it.

Gwenda She won't talk about it though. Says she fell down the stairs. Anyway, listen to me. Do you want a cuppa?

Bridie Sure I thought you'd never ask. Have you got a biscuit?

Gwenda You can give me a hand with the veg too.
They are the first from Tom's allotment.

Both *exit*.

Scene 4: The Widow

SCREEN: Shots of the works and Archie

MUSIC: ACCIDENTS

LYRICS:
There's fourteen men working on the side of a furnace
And the gas creeps up on them like some deadly weed
When the only thing to save them has to be brought from London.
Can saving only ten men compensate for their greed?

Here the accidents are many, no matter how large or small
When one man has gone there's ten more to take his place
Now Corby has its mortuary and the Works it helps to fill it
How many years must pass until somebody cares?

The unions are trying, the Works is getting safer
And mostly we only lose limbs instead of lives
But what about the ghost shift who will never leave here
Will they wander the site long after we've gone?

*Enter **Isa**, a Glaswegian widow, carrying a photo album and a mug of tea. She sits at the table and begins leafing through the album.*

Isa   That's Erchie, ma man. *(His face appears on screen.)* We'd 'a been married 25 years the morra. We came tae Corby frae Glesga when they shut doon the works up there. They sed they needed people fur the joabs.

Why they couldnae ave just built the new works up in Scotland is a mystery tae me. But gnaw - move the people doon tae another country, thousands o' us.

Men first, and then the wumen and wains. What a bloody upheaval. Living withoot yer man, bringing up yer wains on yer ain while he was doon here in a camp with the rest of the men. Nothin' tae dae but drink and fight withoot us wumen tae keep them in order.

No' that they didnae deserve a dram after a hard day's graft in that hell hole. The stories ma Erchie used to tell me. The heat … the thirst … the noise … the accidents!

Well, that's how I lost ma Erchie. He was wan o' the men that fell into the molten steel when the planks gave way. *(Big pause and reflection, looking into space. Refocusing:)* Health and safety? They didnae have safety precautions in them days. They didnae care, men were ten a penny.

Oh, I got a nice letter from Stuarts and Lloyds when he died. But that and the wee drap compensation couldnae replace a faether or gi' me back ma man.

Oh aye, the Works wis guid tae him in many ways. A steady joab wi' a future. Highest-paid work you could find roon here. And he had the best bunch o' pals onywan could ask fur. They wur there fur me and ma wains efter the accident.

But then the whole toon is like that. I suppose we're like wan big clan *(she drags this out.)* Nae matter where you came fae, you'd left a lot behind. Family, friends, your ain hoose, a familiar way of life, even a language. There're enough Scots here to make ye forget that this is England sometimes.

But yu know, up the road no-one ever asks me to slow doon 'cos they canny understand what I'm sayin'.

Why don't I go back? Well, there's nae future fur the wains. Nae joabs.

At least here they'll hae work. Ma Rab's in the tubes and when Alec, ma next eldest, finishes school next year he'll be straight doon the Works.

Tae begin wi' he'll be getting a boy's wage. It won't be till he turns 18 that he gets a man's money, but at least it's another wage coming in.

Ma Fiona will be next. Oh aye she'll hae a choice; no' jis the offices or cleaning. Wumen work on the shop flare as well y'know! Mind you if she cerries on the way she is wi' that young Jamie, she'll be sterting a family before a job.

Just think! Me ... a granny! I'm no' ready fur that. *(Thinks of Archie:)* We used tae talk aboot growin auld taegether. Now he'll never see his grandwains. Aye an' it'll be sad fur them no tae have a grampa. Still! *(Getting up to go:)* Their life will be so different, a lot easier tae oors.

She better no' be expectin' me tae look after they wains! I've got ma own life tae lead noo! Listen tae me bletherin' on. I've things tae do.

Nice talking to you. Cheerie bye!

Isa *bustles off stage.*

Scene 5: The Steelworker

SOUND: Inside a Steelworks

SCREEN: Women in Steelworks, and shots of East Carlton Park and the Lincoln estate

*Enter **Maureen,** a retired Steelworker from Hartlepool.*

Maureen   I was the youngest woman in the Steelworks in Hartlepool. 24, I was. My job was tally-woman. I used to have to lean over and mark the white-hot steel as it came out. I never had any hair at the front of my head 'cos I didn't like to keep the protective cap down over my eyes.

Silly when I think of it now, but back then I had my looks to think about.

I was the last woman to leave too. We women were all being paid off, like after the war. Training up the lads, we were. They were even cheaper than us to employ.

Anyway, how did I come to Corby? My husband applied to be a fuel technologist at Stewarts and Lloyds, and the first I ever heard mention of the place was when he told me he was going for an interview.

He got the job and we came down in 1965. We were offered a staff house here at East Carlton Park. You like them? I'd have gone stir-crazy living out in the sticks. No! I was a townie, so we went for one of the new staff houses on the Lincoln.

Yes, you heard me right! From Sower Leys to Grantham Walk were all staff houses. Snob Hill they called it. Oh, it was state of the art then I can tell you. The architect won awards and all sorts!

"How many women can you condemn to a life of misery" awards. Each of us in solitary confinement, never seeing another soul from day to day. No doorstep culture or over the fence chat … you'd have needed a bloody ladder for that. Six-foot-high fences out the back. I used to sit at my door for hours hoping someone would pass by. No-one ever did. There was nothing to do.

I went to my doctor's, I was that depressed. "Oh!" he said, "the Valium estate," and handed over a prescription. Later they called it the Lincoln Blues.

Back home me and my mum had been in a ladies' club. So, I got to thinking that we needed something like that here. The council gave us a bungalow on Lincoln Way and soon there were two full days of activities.

It wasn't until us women got talking that we realised we were all in the same boat. Not just the isolation, but the lack of facilities, the long haul to the town and back, and the school stuck out in the middle of a field like the Lone Ranger.

So we did something about it. Once we got started, there was no stopping us. We outgrew the bungalow so the council gave us two shop units on Canada Square. Soon we had play groups and one o'clock clubs as well as our social activities, and after three years it became a licensed club. I left the estate for a short time ... but I missed it. Missed the sense of community we'd created. Missed the woods and the lack of traffic. So I moved back.

I've seen it go through some changes. The Maple Leaf, the Square Peg, to the Leaf. Golden Cockerel to The Lincoln. From the day the Canadian High Commissioner came to open Canada Square to the knocking down of the houses on Lincoln Way earlier this year.

Oh yes, the "Valium estate", the worst estate, but I've raised my family here, it's where I live, it's my home.

Scene 6: Cleaners

*Enter **Elsie**, a cleaner, with a mop and bucket. She watches the screen.*

SCREEN: The "Fairer Sex" section from "Double Harvest"

Elsie   Aye, we women did lots of jobs down the Works. All those and on the shop floor too.
Now me, I was one of an army of cleaners. Ever wondered what happens once the boss has gone home?

SCREEN: Shots of the Works to show the scale of the site

*Elsie starts cleaning with a mop. Enter **Cissie**, another cleaner, who joins in. They work in companiable silence.*

Elsie makes tea.

Elsie   I saw Maggie earlier on. She's the size of a house. I reckon she's carrying a boy. It's all at the front.

Cissie   She's lucky to have her mum down here. When I had my first I was alone. Didn't have a clue.

Elsie   We had that long drive over to Kettering too. At least now there is the maternity unit.

Cissie	Thank goodness for that. My cousin lost one of her twins back in 1947 - remember that really cold winter? The roads were all snowed up and by the time they got to the hospital the baby was dead.

*Enter **Mary,** an experienced older cleaner.*

Mary	It's freezing out there. Get the kettle on!
Elsie	I've already made it.
Cissie	Would you not be better doing a bit of work first?
Mary	Oh, I'll get started when me hands are warmed through.
Elsie	Well if you're having tea, I suppose we could join you. *(They all sit around as **Elsie** gets the tea things.)*
Cissie	I'm sure the boss is off home anyway.
Mary	You know there was a new lass on the bus sitting in my seat! Cheek of it!
Elsie	Have you put your money in for Maggie?

| Mary | Not yet, but I'll give it you next week I promise.
Money's a bit tight this week. What did you get her anyway? |
|---|---|
| Elsie | A housecoat like we said ... out of the catalogue. |

*Enter new cleaner, **Sally**, a young woman.*

Sally	Is this the Quantivac?
Cissie	Aye it is, lass. Come in, we don't bite. Are you new?

***Sally** nods her head and hesitantly enters.*

Mary	You're a bit late, aren't you?
Sally	I went to the wrong place.
Mary	How come?
Sally	Well me dad said to just follow the men. So I did ... right into the blooming showers. This one man kindly brought me here in his truck.

*Enter **Mavis**, the supervisor.*

Mavis	*(Sternly:)* So are you lot coming or going?
Mary	Coming.

Elsie	Going.

Cissie	Gone.

Mavis	*(Strolling to shelves to check for dust:)* I sincerely hope you intend to do some work this evening? Perhaps you plan to stay later instead to make up for starting late?

Mavis exits, crossly slamming the door.

Mary	I'd best get started. Are you coming with me? *(To Sally:)* I'll show you the ropes. See you later.

Sally and Mary exit together. Elsie drains her cup then speaks to Cissie.

Elsie	Read my tea leaves before I rinse my cup.

Cissie	*(Gazing for a while:)* Well, I see a bit of a row between you and someone small.

Elsie	Me! I never fall out with anyone. *(She waits eagerly:)* Is that all? Best keep reading that book your daughter got you.

Elsie returns to mopping the floor.
After a short silence she speaks.

Elsie	You know I still do my floors on my hands and knees. I'd love a mop bucket like this. Maybe Santa will remember me for Christmas.
Cissie	There's one out in the yard.
Elsie	Yes, I've seen it.
Cissie	Well, take it home with you.
Elsie	Oh, I couldn't steal it.
Cissie	It wouldn't be theft … it's been out there for ages.
Elsie	Well, how would I clock out with that in my hands?
Cissie	Oh I'll clock you out. I'll meet you outside tomorrow.
Elsie	Would you really! That's awful kind of you. I'll have to walk home though. It's snowing. Just my luck.

*Enter **Mary** and **Sally**.*

Mary	Well that's me finished. I'm off down the canteen for some chips. See you tomorrow.

Hangs up dirty mop and exits.

Cissie	I'm glad I don't have to eat at her table if her home is as clatty as she is!
Elsie	Ach! She means well. Don't do what she does, love. Rinse your mop out in clean water before you finish.

Sally busies herself cleaning her mop. Enter another cleaner, Megan, carrying a bag of wet washing.

Megan	Hello, are you all still here?

She starts unloading a large bag of washing and draping it on the radiators.

Megan	Bloody spin-dryer broke and I'll never get this all dried in this weather.
Cissie	Big Mavis is on the warpath!
Megan	Oh Christ, I thought she'd have gone home by now.
Mary and **Elsie**	So did we!
Megan	Well sod it! I'm sure she's seen a man's long johns before. I'm cleaning over at the coke ovens anyway, so if I'm not here, she won't know whose they are, will she? *(Wipes hands on overall and leaves in a hurry.)*

The others start putting on their coats.

Cissie   Rather her than me!

Elsie   Are you coming with us, lass?
                    We'll show you where to go …
                    avoiding the showers.

Cissie   *(To **Elsie**:)* Aren't you forgetting your
                    bucket?

Elsie   Oh yes… I'll get it now.
                    See you tomorrow. *(Exits.)*

Cissie   *(To **Sally**:)* She'll be changing her name
                    to Liza by tomorrow - that bucket's full
                    of holes!

*Exit **Cissie** and **Sally**, laughing and singing
"There's a hole in my bucket".*

Scene 7: Canteen Worker

*Enter **Jo**, a young worker, sweeping as she goes.*

Jo   Do you know, I've only been working here for six months. But it feels a lot longer. Came straight from school. Why the Plug Mill canteen? Well … I'd failed my "A" levels.

One mate did well and was off to uni. I'd just been to my other friend's wedding and I knew I wasn't ready for that! So, I applied for a job as assistant cook down here at the Works.

I thought it'd be a doddle! How wrong can you be? It is heavy work, and I mean heavy. I suppose I just hadn't thought about the size of everything on an industrial scale. This is just one of many canteens - staff and works.

Anyway, 'cos I'm strong, I get quite a lot of the lifting to do.

I am on 6 to 2 and 2 to 10. I hate 2 to 10. It feels like a waste of a day. Whilst 6 to 2 suits me just fine. Many's the time I've watched the sunrise on my way down Sower Leys Road, after a

172

cracking all-night party up the Lincoln somewhere. I drop in at home and then carry on straight down to the works. Over the flyover, clocking in on the dot of six!

Still in my fur coat, mind, and often with a hangover. I'm sure at the start the older women wondered who I thought I was, swanning around in that. Anyway, handling 24 eggs at a time with a hangover is no mean feat, I can tell you!

And the toaster - I have rows of burn marks on my arms from the grill.
It's the breakfasts I do most. Egg and bacon double-decker. Sausage, egg and bacon double-decker. Egg and sausage double-decker - all on toast.
Big men. Big appetites. Lots of toast.

That's not all we serve. Pie and chips, grey cabbage, mashed potato by the bathful, and puddings. Lottie's homemade soup and puddings.
Apple crumble and custard - gallons of the stuff.

Dropping a huge vat of that into the hot water without trapping your fingers is quite an art, I can tell you. But then there is a lot of skill involved in this job.

I've learned how to wring out a dishcloth properly and how to mop floors. They are so greasy they need soaked first. The older women showed me. They are really helpful and there's some right characters.

Lottie … singing away with the dishcloth tails in her pinny. Norah Sweeney, with her hair all yellow at the front from the nicotine.
Peggy … stuck in that wee kiosk selling cigarettes, sweets, matches. It's no bigger than a tiny cupboard. And Florence Winstanley. 55. The chip fryer. She gave me a lovely garnet ring for helping her with the chips.

Sometimes I have to count the money in the vending machines
or I go on the tills. That's my favourite job. The men send down the apprentices with a big box to get their food. They come themselves if it's overtime. The line is really long, and the meal is free - I take names then, not money. You'd be surprised the number of men with fingers missing.

I met my boyfriend here. He's an apprentice. He'd often sit on his own and sometimes I'd sneak into the kiosk so I could look at him without him noticing. Dark and mysterious. I also work part-time as a barmaid up the Domino. One night he came in and we started talking.

I knew I didn't want to spend my life frying eggs. However good the company. Not that I'm afraid of hard work - but I want to see more of the world. So him and me are off hitching to the South of France.

I got my passport the other week. It was when I wrote "assistant cook" that I decided I wanted more. Next time, I'll write "photographer"!

*Exit **Jo**.*

Scene 8: Interlude
(projection only – audience watch the screen)

SCREEN: Visual script of the town growing

MUSIC: AS THE WORKS GROWS

LYRICS: *(words in bold indicate image change)*

*Down in **Bess**emer and **Kelvin Grove***
*The **houses** they ap**pear***
*Also **East** Carlton where the **staff** live*
*The **diffe**rence it is **clear***
*We **have** the pubs to en**joy** ourselves*
*But **still** nowhere to **pray***
*What we **need** now are some **church**es*
*This **means** we're here to **stay***

Chorus

*The **Cath**olic church now's es**tab**lished*
*It's **going** to ex**pand***
*And the **Scots** have raised six **thou**sand pounds*
*Their **church** it will be **grand***
*But the **bap**tist and congre**gat**ional church*
*They still have far to **go***
*So they'll **meet** in Messrs Lloyds **Cine**ma*
*But they're **bid**ing time you **know***

*With the **church**es, houses, **grave**yards too*
*The **town** it has been **born***
*With the **Scots** in the ma**jo**rity*
*It **did**n't take them **long***
*For **if** you came from **Ste**vie Way*
*It's **jus**t like being **home***
*Now you **live** in little **Sco**tland*
*There **is** no need to **roam**.*

MUSIC: 'COCK O' THE NORTH' - FIDDLE TUNE X 4

Scene 9: Strike Meeting

SCREEN: Canteen slide with headlines about closures

Enter **Narrator**.

Narrator	In February 1979, British Steel announced plans to close the Steel end of the Corby plant with the potential loss of 5,500 jobs. By April that figure was estimated at 12,000. The newly-formed campaign group ROSAC - Retention of Steel at Corby - spearheaded the fight to save Steel, alongside the ISTC and other trade unions.

Enter six 1970s canteen workers. They sit around the canteen.

Elaine	What's this meeting about then?
Annie	Closure, no doubt.
Mary	My man says that's not gonna happen 'cos the union's not said anything official yet.
Jean	When are people gonna wake up? Why are we up and down to London and holding meetings and actions if there is no threat?
Mary	Left-wing troublemakers, the lot of you.

Annie	I was on the last coach to London and I'm no troublemaker. This town relies on the Works and without it there's no future for my kids.
Mary	Talking of troublemakers …

*Enter **Karen**, the union rep. The women greet her.*

Karen	As the ISTC rep, I'm here to explain that we want your support for a national Strike to improve wages throughout the Steel industry. I'm counting on you to come out and make this a solid response.
Jean	Where has the union been while I've been freezing my arse off on the ROSAC stall on a Saturday?
Karen	This isn't about closures, ladies, this is about wages.
Jean	What bloody good is a wage rise if you haven't got a job?
Karen	I agree we need to keep on with our own campaign but this is about the Steel industry nationally. And the tube works is not under threat. We need to stand with them.
Gwenda	They didn't stand with us did they? All the men thought about when we

were out on strike was their sodding stomachs. They didn't take us serious at all.

Isobel   I'll do what my man thinks best. The blast furnacemen reckon we should be accepting closure and already talking about the money.

Elaine   I've got a son in the tubes and a husband in the coke ovens. Which way do I go?

Isobel   Well, my man heard that they'll lose any offer on the table if they come out.

Karen   BSC scaremongering. The redundancy settlement is a separate issue. We've got to think about the future.

Jean   There isn't one if the Works shuts!

Gwenda   If my husband and I both strike now we'll have nothing to live off and no job at the end of it. And I for one have a mortgage to pay for, and we've families to feed.

Annie   Well, I've never crossed a picket line in my life and I don't intend to start now. OK, the Works may be closing, but let's go out with a bang and show "Maggie the milk snatcher" how much the country relies on Steel.

| Karen | Well said - it'll be the miners next if she has her way. Mark my words. So ladies, all those in favour of supporting the strike? |

Very lukewarm response. **Women** *leave muttering.*

| Karen | *(To audience:)* Of course when we first heard about closures, we all stood together. We knew that there would be no future for the town and for our kids. And we thought we could fight it. |

Maureen *joins her.*

| Maureen | The ROSAC committee organized a whole range of events. We lobbied BSC wherever we could find them. There were coaches went down to meet the men who walked to London to hand in the petition. Corby's own Jarrow-style march. And we had days of action. |

| Karen | There was no need to persuade and cajole workers to strike in the September of 1979 when it was decided to bring the whole town to a halt. The walk-out here at the Works was solid. |

| Maureen | The community was right there behind us. Schools brought their students along and mums with babies in prams and pushchairs joined the march. |

Karen	Young and old, united in the simple knowledge that without its heart of Steel, our town would die.
Maureen	The chamber of commerce agreed to close down the town. Nothing moved! Nothing opened. We reckon it was the first time anything like that had happened in this country. A whole town united in defence of its future.
Karen	And we weren't alone. Local unions, like the post office workers and the shop workers came out in support. And miners, dockers, car workers and Steel workers from other towns all came to Corby to show their solidarity.
Maureen	They knew they would be next if the closures went ahead in Corby. The question was: who was next in line?
Karen	The police were on red alert. Remember this was '79. Before Greenham Common and the miners' strike. Before police in riot gear were a common sight. For the union reps to get into the meeting with British Steel they had to get through a cordon of riot police four deep.

Maureen   They needn't have worried. A whole
               town out on the streets and no trouble.
               Exciting times.

Karen   What was it like?

Maureen   We'll show you.

Scene 10: The Demonstration

SCREEN: Images of the 1979 demonstration in Corby, and London march

SET: The table becomes the ROSAC stall

**MUSIC: KEEP THE CANDLE BURNING /
HAPPY TOWN OF STEEL**

Canteen workers and other cast members enter carrying the ROSAC banner and placards as if they have just arrived in London to greet the marchers. They lay out the ROSAC stall.

*Three **Steelmen** enter from stage left. One is the spokesman, **Peter McGowan**. Another is **Monty**. They are greeted warmly by the **Canteen Women**, who take them to meet the crowd, and **Karen** eventually guides him over to the podium.*

Karen   Please welcome our first speaker, Peter McGowan.

Peter   At the end of this long and memorable march, I would like to pay tribute to the Corby public for their long and loyal support during the campaign to save our Steelworks.

I would also like to take this opportunity to thank you on behalf of ROSAC and the marchers for coming here today, to demonstrate to the members of parliament our total opposition to the closure plans and the effect it will have on the town and its people.

I would also like to express our sincere gratitude for the very kind gestures of hospitality we received during our long walk from Trades Councils and the people of Irthlingborough, Rushden, Bedford, Luton, Dunstable, St Albans, and Brent, who made us very welcome, especially the Luton Fire and Paramedic Services who even arranged medical check-ups at a local hospital for us.

Our final challenge is now to meet and present on your behalf this petition to the members of parliament, in the hope that they will recognise that their decision will be catastrophic for Corby.

Let's raise the battle cry, let the politicians know that the Corby people are on their doorstep. Save Steel! Save Corby! Save Steel! Save Corby!

The crowd react very supportively.

*Enter **Maggie Thatcher** with her **two bodyguards,** one of whom is carrying a detonator. The crowd jeer and hiss and is hostile to her.*

Monty	What are you doing here? Why don't you get back to Grantham and sell some more beans, you old fart?

Tension dissolves as the crowd laugh.

Maggie	Thank you for that warm welcome! This is the first demonstration I have ever been on and I assure you it will be my last. *(Aside:)* And theirs too if I have my way.
Monty	We never asked you to come!
Maggie	What is all this shouting and yelling and placard-waving going to achieve?
Monty	Publicity!
Maggie	Do you think we take a blind bit of notice? Of course we don't!
Monty	*(Agreeing with her:)* We've noticed!
Maggie	But we do care.
Crowd	Rubbish!
Maggie	Steel is dead. *(Screen changes to STEELWORKS.)* Who wants to work in heavy industry?
Crowd	We do!

Maggie	We can leave that to men overseas and import what we need.
Monty	What's wrong with BRITISH Steel?
Crowd	Save our Steel! Save our Steel!
Maggie	We promise to find you new jobs, clean jobs, flexible jobs.
Crowd	*(General pandemonium:)* We want the ones we've got!
Maggie	*(Watching, unmoved:)* Oh, so you're not convinced?
Crowd	NO!
Maggie	You say you'll keep on fighting.
Crowd	YES!
Maggie	Very stirring stuff; but you voted for me and my Government!
Crowd	Oh, no we didn't!
Maggie	Oh, yes you did! So, let's get rid of these dinosaurs. Finish the work of my predecessors - *(Points at **Peter**:)* the Labour government!
Crowd	BOO!

Maggie	Make way for the future!

MUSIC: 1812 OVERTURE, CANNONS SECTION (very loud) - TCHAIKOVSKY

Maggie	5, 4, 3, 2, 1!
Crowd	(Chanting loudly:) Save our Steel! NO! Maggie, Maggie, Maggie, out, out, out! (etc.)

As **Maggie** counts down to demolition, newspaper headlines referring to the battle to save the Steelworks appear one after another on the screen, fast-forwarding through time. Then **Maggie** presses the detonator repeatedly, in time to the sound of cannon fire on the soundtrack, synchronised with images on the screen detailing the demolition of the Steelworks. **Monty** rushes at her to try and stop her, but the bodyguards hold him back. He angrily makes as if to leave the stage. He tries to encourage **Peter** to go with him, but **Peter** is overwhelmed by the pointless destruction and is sitting dejectedly holding his Steel hat in his hands.

Monty	(Walking offstage:) You'll not get away with this! We'll keep fighting!

The crowd are devastated, their placards drooping. There is a stunned silence. For the time being, **Maggie** has won. It is important to let the audience really feel the dejection and desolation - to experience the irreparable damage to the community that she did.

The 1812 Overture finishes. There is silence.

Maggie   Well, don't just stand there! Off to the
                   dole queue, all of you. You'll soon find
                   another job!

All exit.

MUSIC: HOT STUFF - DONNA SUMMER

INTERVAL

MUSIC: DRINKING SONG, RESERVOIR SONG

ACT TWO

Scene 1: Wonderworld

The **Pied Piper of Wonderland**, *a character based on both Michael Heseltine and the Pied Piper of Hamelin, enters in front of closed curtains with a red ribbon.*

Pied Piper

Why so glum? I'm your chum
Come with me, you will see
From the ashes you will rise
Like a phoenix, and you'll thrive
Lots of new jobs, clean and smart
Women now can play their part
Enterprise, that's where it's at -
Or Maggie dear will eat her hat!

*Enter **Maggie Thatcher** and her two **Bodyguards**. Between them they perform a ribbon-cutting ceremony. They exit. The curtains open to reveal a row of chairs representing a conveyor belt. A film about Wonderworld is playing on the screen.*

Film Presenter

(On screen:) This is Wonderworld, a £367 million leisure project which its backers say will provide 3,000 jobs. It has received the personal support of Mrs Thatcher.

Group 5, the developers, promise a unique family day out. An all-year-round combination of Disney-style theme park and nursery-rhyme fantasy.

But Wonderworld has seen deadlines come and go, and it remains a plastic model.

With the depression still biting deep, more women are looking for work. Many of Corby's new jobs have gone to them and not the ex-Steelworkers.

An Ex-Steelworker *(On screen:)* I've been up and down here for years now, trying to look for a job, and I haven't found one yet.

Interviewer *(On screen:)* Is it difficult for someone like you to get a job?

Steelworker *(On screen:)* I don't think I'll ever work again, to tell you the truth.

Film clip ends.

Scene 2: Broken Dreams

This scene is a physical theatre depiction of factory work, set to music, with moving images taken from a promotional 1980s CBC video entitled "Corby Works", intercut with Anglia News footage.

*It is 1984. Five of the now-redundant canteen workers from Act One, **Annie**, **Karen**, **Jean**, **Yvonne and Isobel**, are working with other women, **Jan** and **Josie**, in a box factory in Corby's new Enterprise Zone.*

MUSIC: BROKEN DREAMS - BANNER THEATRE - from 1994 play "SWEATSHOP"

During the song, the women enter the Factory dispiritedly, take off their coats, put on work hats and take their place at the conveyor belt. They mime the repetitive, boring, tiring work of assembling boxes.

LYRICS:
It's women's work and we come real cheap
Part-time, part-paid, bottom of the heap
Pin money? Well, that's a joke
Slogging your guts out for one more bloke
Working all day for the capitalist
And then back home to do another shift
No-one noticed the work we did -
Packing and cleaning and raising the kids
The last to be hired and the first to be sacked
Disposable workers off the rack
And the men kept the men's jobs just for the men
While we get the scrag ends all over again

Voice of worker *(on recording:) Every day it's depressing, you see job losses every day on the television, we've been wiped out …*

We worked on your looms and your rolling mills
Toiled in your shipyards to pay our bills
In your deep-seam mines we sweated blood
Night shift, day shift - you screwed us good
Picked your fruit and ploughed your land
Built power stations and hydro dams
Schools, hospitals, motorways
We sold our life's blood to earn our pay
Now you're pulling out, the future's gone
To Seoul, Jakarta, Beijing, Taiwan
God save the queen and the union jack
Like the factory gates, we're up for scrap.

Voice of worker *(on recording:)* You have to have 4 "O" levels now to be a Dustbin Man.

We laboured with craft, we laboured with skill
Now we queue at the job club with time to kill
Jobs on security now and again
Chicken pluckers or lollipop men
You can train to wash dishes, you can train to clean
Or be a brain surgeon on some bloody scheme
When the training's done it's "sorry, chuck
No jobs here, shove off, tough luck!"
Ten quid a day, no holiday pay
No cards, no Union, no bloody way!
We've sold our lives to the big machine
And we're left with nothing but broken dreams
Broken dreams, broken dreams.

*The **Women** turn to the screen.*

Voices of workers *(on recording:)* £3.60 an hour ... paid buttons for money ... £2.75 per hour ... buttons for money ... £2.05 ... £2.05 ... that is disgusting ... £1.74 an hour ... below Union rates ... 40p a skirt ... Union rates ... 10p for putting a zip on ... disgusting ... 2600 rupiahs a day ... treated like dirt ... one dollar a quarter ... treated like dirt ... 6p an hour ... minimum wages ... 0.3 pence per solder joint - that is disgusting ... disgusting!

Corby Councillor Tom Mackintosh *(on film:)* I think you'll find ... a lot of people in the town ... especially unemployed people are looking for - not cheap jobs ... not jobs with low pay ... they're looking for a future.

*The **Women** get their coats, and then rearrange chairs for the next scene to suggest a room where they have come for their break. They chat naturally and eventually sit down.*

Scene 3: The Aftermath

This scene is an unbroken continuation of Scene 2, with everyone remaining in place.

Jean

We haven't got long.

Jan

I've had a reply from the Miners' Wives Support Group in Castleford, West Yorkshire, to say we can come up next weekend.

Jean

Read it, then.

Jan

(Reads letter:)
"Dear Sisters, you would be very welcome to come and talk to us about how you have survived since the closure of the Steelworks. We are having a do next Saturday, as it looks like both Glass Oughton and Lekston Luck Pits are on the hit list for closure. Thanks for your support and your kind donations. We are taking the kids to Scarborough on a trip with the money.
In solidarity, Susan Perry, Secretary, Castleford Miners' Wives Support Group."

So, we better practise what we want to say!

Jean

Go on then, you first.

Women take it in turns to get up as if on stage and practise what they will say to the miners' wives.

Karen   Four years on and where have we got to? Men at home watching TV or down the pub. Being expected to adapt to making the dinner instead of making Steel. Self-esteem gone. Their role as breadwinner ... provider ... man - changed forever. Whilst we women work all the hours that God sends, for some cowboy firm who'll just up sticks and move when their subsidy has run out.

Jobs for women a-plenty. The boss gets away with part-time hours and pays us less - any hint of Union organisation and you're out the door. And none of us will fight it 'cos we're too desperate to hold down the job.

The Workers' Rights Group is leafleting outside the factories trying to get a foothold. But the Unions have been silenced since the Works closed. Left out of the discussions about bringing jobs to the town. We don't want jobs at any price! We want secure jobs - new jobs, not ones just moved here from elsewhere.

The Union was a way of life down the Works. There was a whole support network ... and benefits ... and community - a safety net. Now it is everyone for themselves. I'm all right, Jack! Divide and rule.

Jean

Of course - Maggie's started on the miners now. Her ... and that butcher Ian McGregor. It'll be the dockers next! We know what it's like to have the guts ripped out of your community. The least we can do is give our support. You were there for us when we needed you. Return the favour! Stand together! I'm out collecting food for the striking miners most nights. And we women have started a committee to bring miners' kids here for a holiday.

I remember the Steel Strike as if it was yesterday. And I bet there's the same family battles going on as we had. There're brothers who still don't speak even now. It's the principle! I can't believe people don't understand the need for solidarity ... but I suppose everyone had their own valid reasons for doing what they did. It was hard to manage without any money ... despite the food parcels and bags of veg from the wholesalers. I remember my Frank took a parcel round to one striker.

Older lady ... on her own ... no family support. And the following week we heard she'd killed herself. Pulled the electric fire in the bath with her.

It's the selfish bastards I don't understand ... the ones who never even tried. The boss's darling! I hope the miners realise that redundancy pay - no matter how many noughts they put on the end of it - runs out eventually ... and you're left with nothing - no industry and no future.

Annie
It's the kids I worry for. By the time they leave school, the whole idea of a proper job, a job for life - comrades, workmates, common trades and skills to bind you together - will have gone. Call that progress? It's gone backwards - not forwards. Back to the days of the dockers standing in pens on the docks waiting to be picked for a day's labour.

These new agencies are a rip-off! They get a huge profit for every worker they send on a thirteen-week trial. No ties for the employer. No sick pay, holiday pay, maternity pay - no security! My pal went for an interview at one place that had 3,000 applicants for seventy jobs! They expect you to be available for work at the drop of a hat.

There's plenty of work on these new twilight shifts. Mind you - that's when the kids are in and home from school. And unless your man is on the dole and will watch them while you go out to work, it's back to latchkey kids … The pair of you out working, and the kids left to their own devices. Bringing themselves up, they were. No wonder there's all this "drugs and teenage mums."

Josie   My man went for retraining - he's nearly done as an accountant. Sometimes I have to pinch myself. What a journey! From blast-furnace man using his bulk, body and brawn - he's a big man, is my Ernie - to an accountant! I'm surprised that he still has a brain left to do it with, after the amount of drinking he did with all that redundancy pay. Nearly split us up, it did.

Well, I'd just finished a degree myself. I was sick of being thought of as thick, so I went back to school. I graduated the day the closure was announced! Brought up my three children and then decided it was my turn. I thought I'd be able to find a decent job that paid more than the pin money we get here. We don't even get equal pay. And you can forget graduate employment.

They see Corby folk as factory fodder. So much for getting an education to better yourself. I'm worried he'll not get a job at the end of his course either. I mean ... surely accounting is a middle-class profession. How the hell will he find the experience - the contacts! I hoped this would give him a better control of the family purse - but no - it still falls to me to balance it up.

Elaine   At least she's got something to balance up. My Johnny got £30,000 redundancy money. He invested it - in the bloody bookie's. Lost the lot. So it's me out earning the wages now, and the lazy bugger won't lift a finger to help in the house. The gambling's nothing new. He's always done it. We've never had a penny. Folk used to look down on us. But we're every bit as good as they are. I remember when we women would get a bus on a Friday at 12 o'clock - specially laid on, down to the wages office - to stand and wait with your hands open, to make sure your man coughed up the wages before he got down the pub or the bookie's. Some of them used to be too ashamed to go home after going on a bender and spendin' it all - so they'd go back and sleep on the shop floor, tell the wife they were doing overtime.

The other men would bring in food
and sure enough ... they'd work like
a navvy to make up some pay. Many
a couple came to blows about the
wages being pissed up against the wall.
Saturday night up the Labour Club. *(She
remembers.)*

It wasn't unheard-of for people to go
off with someone else - ships passing in
the night at home - and it was lonely,
so you sought comfort where you could
get it. Silly buggers wouldn't be able to
keep their mouths shut though, and they
would go into work bragging about it.
But that's men for you!

Yvonne   OK, let's talk about the money - how
do you go from tipping up what's left
of your wages to handling thousands?
The banks have moved in here like
sharks - offshore banks, Irish banks ...
Some men did invest wisely. Like my
Robert. We bought our house, and I
had my last child knowing it had a roof
over its head. Some of my neighbours
just disappeared - couldn't keep up the
payments. Moonlighting, they called it.
Put the keys to the house through the
estate agent's door and headed off to a
new life somewhere else.

I reckon the Works closing was a godsend to some men. They had a chance to set up as self-employed. Be their own boss. A good few went out on the taxis. And they'll all be in work once they start on that Wonderworld. It'll be great for the kids.

The place looks different too, with all these clean, shiny new factories. I do miss the Corby Candle, though. My youngest used to watch that at night before she went to sleep. But I don't miss the dirt. My washing's a lot cleaner now, I can tell you!

Isobel My man's make-up pay ran out last year. He still has no chance of a decent job here. So, he's off to Holland, where his mate tells him jobs are ten a penny. Imagine, British workers ending up as immigrant labour! Mind you - the pay's better ... and the conditions! And at the end of the day, we were all immigrants here in Corby.

My daughter's just come back from her travels and the first thing she noticed was the number of new X-reg gold Ford Granadas ... And the houses - extensions, porches, conservatories, own front door! The town is changing, that's for sure.

Affluence on the one hand … whilst other areas are virtually derelict.

Mind you … you can buy flats and houses in those areas for next to nothing. Some people have bought two or three and converted them to amazing living spaces. And not just those with redundancy money to spare! People are still coming to Corby for a chance at a better life. One man up the Lincoln came down from Glasgow looking for work. Seven thousand men on the dole! But he was lucky. He got a job - on the buses. Lived in a caravan and as soon as he had money put by, he bought two properties on Blenheim Walk - a real no-go area - and did them up. His own sprawling urban palace. The family joined him as soon as it was ready.

To him it was paradise. He told me he was from Muggers' Alley in Glasgow. So, however much we think the town is going downhill, it is as full of opportunity as ever.

Scene 4: Sweatshop

*The women rearrange the chairs to suggest a bank of industrial sewing machines. Now playing different workers - **Susan**, **Margaret**, **Betty**, **Lizzie**, **Joy**, **Irene** and **Evelyn** - they mime working in a dismal sewing factory whilst a **Supervisor** monitors them closely.*

SCREEN: Images of global sweatshops

MUSIC: SWEATSHOP - BANNER THEATRE - from 1994 play "SWEATSHOP"

LYRICS:
Chorus: Working in a sweatshop, bottom-line wages
Down on the factory floor
Working in a sweatshop, non-stop rip-off
Ain't gonna take no more!

Acid and grime, double overtime
Stinking fumes all the day
Hands in a rash trying to earn my cash
Burning my life away
Just do the job, don't open your gob
Plenty more where you came from
The more you sweat, the less you get
Smethwick, Dundee, Taiwan.

Chorus

Two pounds an hour, working for this shower
Stuck like a dog in a ditch
Non-stop grind, killing my mind
To keep this boss-man rich.

Don't want a Union - says it's gonna ruin him
He ain't gonna pay a penny more
He's in clover, in his big Rover
That's how the poor stay poor.

Chorus - Instrumental break

Hey there Jimmy man
What you gonna gimme man?
You ain't gonna get your way
No more enslavement
We're out on the pavement
And we are here to stay!
Aggravation, intimidation
Down on the picket line
Scabs won't break us
Cops won't shake us
Come sun, rain or shine!

*Fed up with the **Supervisor**'s nit-picking, the women take
an unscheduled break. They re-gather outside the Factory
as the music fades out, and ad lib their complaints about
the **Supervisor**.*

*Enter **Ellen**, the Union rep.*

Ellen   Ladies, can I have your attention? I've
                   just had a meeting with the managing
                   director and he says there is not enough
                   money to pay your wages this week -
                   and the state this company is in, I think
                   we're heading for another redundancy.

Susan	I've been made redundant three times in five years. It's not happening again. I've had enough!
Margaret	What are we meant to live off?
Betty	*(Entering from the factory:)* There's something fishy going on. I've just seen some of the lads carrying some big bits of machinery to a van out the back.
Ellen	What did I tell you!
Jean	What are we going to do about it?
Lizzie	We could run it better ourselves.
Joy	That's a bloody good idea. Why don't we?
Irene	We could have a sit-in.
Ellen	If we took over the factory, they couldn't take the machinery or make us redundant.
Evelyn	*(Indicating **Ellen**:)* There are only the two of us on the Works Committee. We'll need more than that to organize a sit-in.
Lizzie	*(To **Evelyn**:)* I'll join you. I'll sort out food and a cleaning rota.

Evelyn	Anyone else?
Betty	Yes, I'll sort out getting the kids collected from school.
Ellen	*(To **Evelyn**:)* Are you taking notes?
Margaret	If we're staying the night, I'll get my Robert to bring us in a tele and a radio.
Irene	I'll get Eric to sort us some beds. He runs the Scouts. And I'll get someone to go round and get all our bedding and personal things.
Ellen	I'll contact the Union. We'll need their support.
Betty	I'm off to stop those lads taking the stuff. They need to be with us, guarding the machinery - not getting rid of it.
Irene	*(To **Betty**:)* I'll come with you.
Joy	Right, let's go.
Ellen	Wait a minute! Legally, we can't do this. The managing director is still on the premises.

Joy   *(Sarcastically:)* Well, let's invite Mr Azimi to take a break. He never bothered striking up a working relationship with us. He forgets we're human beings. Anyone fancy coming with me to kick him out?

Ellen   I'll come with you.

They all re-enter the factory and line up facing the audience with arms crossed.

SCREEN: Film clip - excerpt from *Anglia News* report, September 1984

News Reporter   *(on film:)* When last week's wages weren't paid, workers say it became clear that the project would fold and they would be left without jobs or redundancy money. A sign outside the factory states: "THIS FACTORY IS *CONTROLLED* BY THE NATIONAL UNION OF TAILORS AND GARMENT WORKERS". Today it's business pretty much as usual, with office staff doing the paperwork, and all the 62-strong workforce staying on. Workers are confident that orders will continue to pay their wages, but they are hoping for a buyer to take on them, the machinery - and their customers. The Union is confident that the company is viable and they say they have had several enquiries about it.

Colin Tindley, Union Official of the NUT and GW *(on film:)* Well, within the last hour we have been visited by a prospective employer. I've told him the worst that he could know because I don't want anybody to be caught by surprise - and he is showing a very keen interest. We are arranging for the owners of the machinery to rush here now, so we can arrange a meeting with them.

News Reporter *(on film:)* The workers are convinced that they can make a go of things. They say that all they need is the finance and good management to secure their future.

Union Rep *(on film:)* Everybody concerned with the factory, and even the past owners, are pleased that we did it. The machinery is safe. Nothing is going to leave here without us knowing.

End of film clip.

MUSIC: WONDERWORLD (REPRISE)

LYRICS:
Here we are, it's a new decade -
Guess what is the news?
The Council's issued an ultimatum
For what have they to lose?
We want to see some building done
For we must now save face
But will the contractors ever listen to them?
Everyone watch this space.

Welcome to Wonderworld
Welcome to Wonderworld
Welcome to Wonderworld
Welcome to Wonderworld

May the first has come and gone -
No builders have moved in
The Council's pulled the plug on them
Now British Steel are set to win
For the land they sold ten years ago
They can buy back for a song
Now with a profit of a hundred million pounds
You can hear the board sing along

Goodbye to Wonderworld
Goodbye to Wonderworld
Goodbye to Wonderworld
Goodbye to Wonderworld

All exit.

ACT THREE

Scene 1: The Steel Kids

*Enter **Narrator**. In the original production, this piece was depicted through physical theatre performed by younger cast members, accompanying the **Narrator**'s delivery.*

Narrator   There's a spirit in this town
Which comes from the Steel.
A recipe for resistance.
From the ore
Dug from the bowels of the earth,
Molten, burned and beaten into shape
A smooth, shiny, indestructible tube
emerges.
We take the knocks, the blows, the
hammering.
The fire rages within.
Stops us fitting, accepting the crumbs.

Some give the knocks, the blows, the
hammerings.
They become famous:
CORBY KEEP OUT!
Not for the faint-hearted!

The Works is gone -
No-one bothers to tend the Steel now.
The tubes is always under threat:
But the ore remains,
And the fire!

Give us the right treatment and we will
endure
And emerge as the best and most
resilient there is.

Leave us as the raw stuff
And the alchemy will never tame the
rage.

Add to that our Celtic roots -
Race memory of domination -
And maybe you'll understand...

The Steel Kids!

Scene 2:
A Chocolate Factory in Corby, 1998

*Enter **Emma** and **Jo**, two women in their early 20s, meeting outside the chocolate factory on their break. **Jo** is about to light a cigarette.*

Emma	What you doing out here? Thought you quit?
Jo	I did. I mean … I'm going to …
Emma	Yeah, right!
Jo	It's no use. I can't make it through these twilight shifts without one!
Emma	I know. Me too. Can't afford it when I'm back at uni though …
Jo	I actually look forward to the break from home, even if it is at a bloody factory!
Emma	So how is the little one?
Jo	He's fine. Teething, bless him. Which is mum-speak for crying all the time!

*Both laugh. Enter **Jen**, another young woman.*

Jo	Bloody hell! Look what the cat dragged in!
Emma	Hi Jen! Haven't seen you for ages!

Jen	Hello girls! The Jenmeister is back in town!
Emma and **Jo**:	Again!

All laugh.

Emma	You run outta money then?
Jen	Yup. What? You think I'd be in this shit-hole if I was flush?
Jo	Watch it! Some of us are here full-time!
Emma	Speak for yourself! Holidays are enough for me. I can't wait to get back to uni …
Jo	So where've you been this time? It wasn't somewhere hot, that's for sure! You've got a Corby tan. *(She laughs.)*
Jen	I've been to Iceland.
Jo	My mum goes there every Saturday. They do great meal deals.

Jen and Emma groan.

Emma	How's your mum, Jen?

Jo nudges Emma. Jen looks uncomfortable and turns to the audience. Jo and Emma freeze-frame during Jen's speech.

Jen	*(To audience:)* I remember the first time I went away. It was to a refuge in Wellingborough. Not quite the trip of a lifetime. Of course, you always have to come back from these places. It must have stuck with me from an early age. If things get too much you can just get up and go - to a refuge, to another town, and things will be great for a while. Until he found us - and then it was back to "normal life". Back to the reality of a violent, alcoholic dad and a scared mum who couldn't cope.
	But if you go that little bit further … people can't find you. You can be free and do the things you never could. And you can change your whole character. Nobody knows your past. You don't have to tell them anything. I can be happy Jen, always travelling 'cos she wants to see the world and experience everything. Instead of THAT Jen with THAT dad. Jen who was found in the streets in her nightie, looking for her mum. Jen who is looking for answers to the questions that can't be answered. I'd still rather be travelling than be here though. I come back when I run out of money. Spend time with my mum. I feel a bit guilty for leaving her. Go straight to the agencies, work all the shifts I can. There's no loyalty on their part or mine. It's great. I get to work the system.

Then, when I get enough money, I get out my map, close my eyes and let fate decide where I'm off to next.

Dad bought me that map when I was little. Half the places on it don't even exist any more! That was when things were OK. When we were a normal family and he had a job and we did normal things! It's scary how you can love someone as much as you hate them. That's why I keep the map. He'd wanted to travel. Was just about to leave when the Works closed - so he never got the chance. Grandad needed his support. It was hard for his family to adjust to life on the dole. And I kinda pity him ...
He ruined his life - and my mum's. But in a messed-up way it forced me to do something with mine. I have experienced so much. This town keeps people here. I wouldn't be the person I am if I'd stayed here. But I wouldn't be the person I am without it either.

I'll do whatever it takes to keep me travelling, till I find somewhere I want to stay. And if that means packing chocolates for a few months ...
(Shrugs:) At least I can leave when I want to ...

*(To **Jo** and **Emma**:)*	So, are you still allowed to eat as many of these as you want?
Jo	Give it a few days, love, and you won't want any for the rest of your life!

***Emma** and **Jen** freeze-frame during the following speech.*

Jo	*(To audience:)* What they don't realise is that I eat them at home as well. Why? Boredom. It's no fun bringing up kids on your own, you know! I'm really jealous that she's been travelling again. It's been years since I had a holiday and even then, it was only to Calais with the school. I had my first hangover on that trip - I still can't drink whiskey!
	I got pregnant not long after we got back. It pretty much put an end to any desire I had to go travelling. A night out is still a luxury! Literally every penny I have earned since I turned 16 has gone on the girls. I don't blame them though. It's not their fault their dad doesn't give us any money. Don't get me wrong - my family have really helped over the years. They supported us financially as well as being there for babysitting and cheering me up. I don't understand how single mothers manage without a family to help them. But most people in Corby have a big family - or a community at

least. That's the best thing about this town, community. Everyone from Corby is an outsider. They all came here for the Works and no-one belonged here, so they built up these little groups, then the Works shut and they came together as a town to fight, and now Corby is more about the people than the place. Which is a good job, 'cos there's not much here to do.

It's no wonder we're all having babies so young - you have to find your own fun in Corby! It's a different story once the boys realise how much hard work having a family is though, they're all talk until responsibility kicks in. Craig didn't leave us straight away, but I think that had more to do with not wanting other people to think bad of him.

Instead, he just started doing everything wrong. Never held down a job and spent all of our money on drugs, fags and Special Brew. Not that there were many jobs to hold down in the years after the Works shut down. I don't know, the older I get, the more I think that he really was too young to start a family. He just couldn't handle the stress of never making ends meet, and we both knew that no matter how hard we tried, things were never going to be that great for the girls.

I'm still trying my best for them. We have a lot of fun exploring the pretty bits all around Corby, like the woods, East Carlton Park and the boating lake. My Jade loves feeding the ducks. Hopefully we'll get a cinema again, and some more stuff to do! It's hard enough finding a babysitter and the money to be able to go out - but then to have to travel to the next town to do it! I don't really bother. I go to my local and have a few drinks and that'll do me. For now. Dad tries to give me money to go out but I'd rather it got spent on nappies. Anyway, I feel bad taking his money. He earns less than me at the minute!

Besides, there comes a point when you need to do it all on your own. I don't want to be living off them - I want to prove that, even though I'm a young single mum, I can look after us by myself. And I do. And it's hard, but we'll get by.

I never thought I'd end up working in a chocolate factory. I had wanted to be a teacher, but you can't take a baby to university. Maybe when my Amy goes to school next year I can think about it, do it part-time. That's if I can afford the fees!

They don't make it easy to better yourself, do they? And I'd have to go somewhere else to do it - nearly four hours a day on the bus is a bit much, and I can't really move. So I'll probably end up just staying here with the kids. I do wonder what life would be like without the girls - but they didn't ask to be born, and it's not their fault I've got such bad taste in men. I'm mostly happy with the way things are, here with my family, in Corby.

*(To **Jen** and **Emma**:)* We'd best be getting back. Some of us can't afford to lose our jobs.

Jen	I'd better nip to the loo!
Emma	I'll be there in a minute!

*Exit **Jo** and **Jen**.*

Emma	*(To audience:)* There's no way I could do this full-time. It would do my head in. They say that goldfish only grow as big as the size of the tank they're in. Corby always felt to me like a very small goldfish bowl. I wasn't comfortable being stunted. I always knew that I needed to do more than just stay in Corby and work a crap job in a factory. And I definitely wasn't going to raise my children here! I mean, what chance would they have in life, growing up in

this tiny, stagnant pond? Imagine what would have happened to us all if we had a big lake full of life. How big we'd have all grown then!

I suppose it wasn't that bad at first. I wasn't really aware that Corby was different to any other town until I was old enough to go out with my friends. The shops used to be OK. We went to the swimming baths every week and would chat in the café afterwards. All that exercise, followed by chips and four bars of chocolate! We had a cinema then too. I went on a date when I was fourteen to see "The Lion King"! I cried during that and had to pretend I had something in my eye … Oh, and the Quasar Laser! That was great!

But it didn't last very long. The cinema went. The Quasar went. Shops shut down and were replaced by card shops! What's that all about? How many cards does one town need? We did end up spending hours in Clintons reading all the jokes though. Well, you've got to keep yourself amused somehow! It's funny, but looking back on those times it was a blessing in very heavy disguise that my stepfather was so strict. I was so scared that I would be caught out doing something wrong that I never sought my amusement in parks with bottles of cider or worse, drugs. It's no wonder so many kids went off the rails. Not many had the money to get to Kettering with its shops and the Odeon and Kettering Leisure Village, and besides it took too long to get there. What were the kids supposed to do with all that pent-up energy? Mix that with teenage hormones and curiosity, and it's a recipe for disaster.

We started to get a reputation. Corby kids! Hard. Mean. Violent. Always looking for trouble. Always looking for something to do, more like! Or guidance!

It wasn't just bad kids that got into trouble. I knew so many kids from good homes that ended up getting arrested. Gang warfare all over the town, fighting about turf. And no one tried to stop the fighting after what happened to Louise Allen. We had police escorts after school when that happened! "You got one of ours, now we're gonna get one of you." You'd think it would have made people stop and think, but it only got worse. Someone always has to pay in this town. It's a never-ending cycle of blame and violence.
I began to hate everything about living here. The town had a really oppressive feel about it. I mean, we feature at

the top of all the statistics - teenage pregnancy, illiteracy, depression, alcoholism and mental health problems. Some legacy!

Aspiration was not a word recognised by my peers. I was lucky. I came from a family who believed in the value of education and would regularly tell me that any dream was within my reach. "They can't take what's inside your head", my grandad used to say. Conflicting messages came from my stepdad, who suffered with depression. He thought I should aim a little lower and that I had too much imagination. He tried to bring me back down to earth. Where apparently our careers advisor lived! I was discouraged from trying to follow any kind of creative route. Office work was OK. Aside from my complete lack of computer skills, you mean?

But Grandad was right. You can't take knowledge and dreams and ambition away. Not if you believe in them. And I did. I still do. I worked hard at school. I knew my only route out of Corby was via university. And then they scrapped the grants system the year before I went. I knew so many people who wanted to go but couldn't afford it. Means-testing worked for me. I don't have to pay fees but it meant I had to get a student loan.

Debt. What a great start in life! But I'm out there. Living my dream. A little fish in a big pond. And I love it! *(She exits.)*

Scene 3: Look to the Future

*Enter **Younger cast members**, who speak in unison.*

Youngsters   Look to the future
Gleaming and bright
Though we've no Corby Candle
To light up the night
But a chance to improve it
A chance it can grow
Into somewhere we're proud of
Like you used to know.
When coming from Corby
Was no badge of shame
But a proud town of Steel
To which everyone came
Who was looking for work,
For a house, for a life.
From all over the world
For a break from the strife
Of communities lacking
The things that we had.
Looking at it like that
Who says Corby's bad?
We're your hope for the future
So please get it right
Build a town we'll be proud of
Rekindle the light
That once welcomed all comers
To old Corby Town.

*Enter **Older Women**, who speak in unison.*

Older Women   No Wonderworld this time
Please don't let them down.
The Steel Kids of Corby
And all those who are new
Would do well to remember
What we've all lived through.

MUSIC: GIVE US A JOB TO DO – THE OREBITS

All sing:

We've made this town our home
Children and families
Built it on hopes and dreams,
Built it on iron ore
Now that we've come of age
Give us what is our due
Pay us a living wage in Corby.

Descant:
Give us something now
Some hope for a future
So our children will have a chance
In Corby.

All exit

CURTAIN

About Her
by
Paula Boulton

**First performed at the ARC Theatre,
Corby, on 12th March 2010**

Synopsis

About Her is based on interviews with a random selection of Corby women in 2008 and gives a flavour of their diverse lives and experiences. The characters start the day in their own homes, giving us a glimpse behind their public faces. They then all find their way to the Lakelands charity shop in the centre of town. En route, and at the shop, there are lots of different conversations as the women interact. Some share their stories with Patrice who is collecting tales for the Talking Books project; others chat together at the bus stop. We also meet a group of five teenage girls who show how different life is for their generation.

Notes for the Director

In several scenes the cast are all busy doing something individually and there is no one action more important than the other. Similarly, there are moments of improvised group chat where no one strand of the conversation predominates. The intention is for members of the audience to focus on whoever or whatever takes their interest. The effect is to present a variety of lives being observed and occurring in parallel.

At other moments one story or character comes to the fore. At those times it is up to the director to bring that out. In the original production this was achieved by lighting and designating one area as the storytelling spot. At other times, the cast were directed to mime silent conversations to allow one particular exchange to be heard. Staggered entrances at the beginning and end allow focus to be given to each woman in turn before the next one is added to the mix.

Though much of the play is scripted, the technique used with the cast was for them to learn their character's life story and to relay stories naturally, rather than to learn a script.

In line with this approach, sometimes the key points of the story are listed rather than given as a verbatim script. Since some of the women were telling their own real-life stories, it was sufficient to simply write, for example, "Hoop story". Similarly, there is sometimes an instruction to talk about something rather than an actual script. Again, this improvised natural dialogue kept the piece alive as it was never quite the same twice in a row, e.g. "**Milica** *is rude about her being a boring old woman.*"

This is slightly different for the teenage girls who take these roles. They are free to create their own characters and backstories, as long as the five they portray show a variety of issues facing girls their age: e.g. lack of confidence and self-esteem, body shaming, need for acceptance, or levels of strictness in different families.

Full character notes on the women can be found in the earlier version of *About Her*, which was first performed as a play reading where all the characters discussed many of the topics which come up in the stage play version. For example, domestic violence, reasons for being in Corby, attitudes to sex and contraception, or fashion. Where necessary, monologues and notes from the interviews with the actual women have been included to allow for improvised dialogue to be built around their testimonies.

The first performance was also in a theatre which had curtains and a wide enough apron to allow scenes to happen there while the set was being changed. The main set for Act One Scene 4 was a local charity shop linked to the Lakelands Cancer Care Hospice. It had a café, book area, bric-a-brac area, clothes rails and a changing cubicle. As long as these functions can happen in your set, it could be set somewhere else which may have a local resonance for your community. The volunteer character was based on a real person.

Characters in Order of Appearance

Ada A Lesbian mother who escaped DV (domestic violence) by coming to Corby

Gaida An older Latvian woman. Been in Corby since 1950

Katerina A newly arrived DV survivor from Poland

Catherine A middle-class retired English teacher and JP

Milica A Serbian mother of two toddlers. In Corby for love

Linda An English DV survivor, newly emerged from a controlling relationship

Morag Feisty Glaswegian, in charge of the charity shop

Karen Young Corby woman, fundraiser for the charity

Alma An original Corby villager. No nonsense

Bronagh Talkative, opinionated, lively Irish woman

Bernadette Quiet, reserved Catholic Irish woman

Patrice An evacuee from Montserrat working for Talking Books

Maggie A hard-working loving Scots woman. Gran to **Cathy**

Five teenage girls - Abby, Caitlin, Cathy, Elle, Ellie - All schoolfriends

ACT ONE

Scene 1: Private Life

MUSIC: SHE - ELVIS COSTELLO

SET: Various simple rooms in houses to match what the women do

The women enter at ten-second intervals and mime their own story. One is sitting at a dressing-table putting on make-up. Another is looking at a bookshelf and selecting books. Another is getting twins dressed and putting them in a pushchair. Another is feverishly hoovering. Each woman can improvise her own version of this section in line with her own characterisation and backstory. This is the private self which she doesn't show to the world.

MUSIC FADES

Scene 2: Bus Stop

SET: A bus stop and bench

*Enter **Morag** and **Maggie**. They stand.*

*Enter **Bernadette** and **Bronagh**. They sit.*

Bernadette:	Morning, Morag, I haven't seen you in ages.
Morag:	Where are you off to?
Bernadette:	We're off up town shopping.
Bronagh:	I'm looking for a special outfit for tonight.
Maggie:	Well, why not drop into Lakelands. We have some really classy outfits at the moment.
Bronagh:	I need something pretty sexy. He's a fine thing.

***Maggie** and **Morag** exchange looks.*

Bernadette:	*(Acting as the peacemaker:)* Ah, we'll pop in for a cup of tea later.

*Enter five noisy teenage girls all loudly discussing homework and their plan to go out to a club called Storm that night. They will have to dress up to look old enough to get in, and are talking about what they are going to wear and who they fancy. **Ellie** walks on, listening to music on* *her mobile phone through earphones, and ignores them whilst singing along loudly.*

Women have their own reactions in silence and mime.

Ellie*'s phone rings and she steps away to take the call.*

Ellie: Hey babe. Yeah, I'm OK, just waiting for the bus. Oh my god. No way. Behind a bush. She has a bush. Ha-ha. I can't believe it. OK, I'll pass it on. *(She immediately texts her friends and walks back across stage.)*

Abby: Are you coming Storm tonight?

Cathy: My mum won't let me.

Caitlin: Tell her you're gonna stay at mine for a sleepover instead.

All their phones ring at the same time.

Ellie: That'll be from me, but I will tell you in person. *(Others listen keenly:)* Well, you know Michaela.

Caitlin: Michaela …

Ellie and **Caitlin:** Blonde hair - big tits.

Abby: Yeah.

Ellie:	Well, she shagged James Porter, behind a bush … *(Girls laugh.)* Oh, and she has a bush. And it's ginger.
Ellie:	*(Pulls out headphone:)* What! Who has a ginger bush?
Cathy:	Michaela.
Abby:	Too much Irn Bru, I think. *(Girls laugh.)*
Morag:	*(Approaching the girls crossly:)* Cathy - you better not let your mum hear you carrying on like that in the street … That's disgusting.
Cathy:	Oh! Hi Gran. You won't tell her, will you?
Morag:	What a way to behave.
Abby:	Don't worry … I'll keep her in line … remember me? I met you at her party. *(**Cathy** tries to get her friends to back off.)*
Cathy:	Can I meet you from work and go and get some new shoes?
Morag:	If you behave yourself.
Cathy:	Thanks Gran! *(Hugs her and runs back to her friends)*
Caitlin:	You're going to get lovely shoes … from Bonmarsh. *(Girls laugh.)*

Elle:	So, what are we doing tonight?
Caitlin:	Oh look, there's Chris and his hunky mates … come on. (*Grabs **Abby** with her as she runs*).

Cathy and ***Elle*** *follow.* ***Ellie***, *listening to her music, notices after a while and runs after them.*

Maggie:	What a carry-on.
Bernadette:	Weren't we all the same at their age?
Maggie:	I certainly wasn't.
Bronagh:	Yeah, we were! Did you never go dancing when you were young?
Bernadette:	We used to cycle to the dances in all weathers. I didn't like dancing in shoes, so I used to sneak out my dinky sandals behind my mum's back.
Bronagh:	When would that have been?
Bernadette:	The late fifties.
Bronagh:	By the mid-seventies we'd get a lift in, in a car. But we'd have to make our own way back. There was me, in my miniest of miniskirts, having to pull a bloke with a car to get home again.
Maggie:	And your mother let you go out like that?

Bronagh:	I was covered from head to toe in a maxi coat - so she wouldn't have realised. *(Laughs.)*
Maggie:	Well, that's as may be. But unlike those little tarts, I certainly wouldn't have spoken about *it* in the street. Sex was taboo when *I* was a girl. Nobody *ever* spoke about it.
Bernadette:	Well, I grew up on a farm, and I learned all about *it* from the farm animals.
Bronagh:	Well, I learned about *sex* from that book "Lady Chatterley's Lover". It was banned this side of the world then, but we managed to get a copy from America.
Morag:	I got "Lady Chatterley's Lover" from a woman at work and I can remember the excitement of reading a bit every night. I hid it under my mattress. Just my luck that my dad came over all helpful and helped my mum with the spring cleaning by turning the mattresses. I found it on top of my bed one day when I came in from work. I thought I'd get a thump, but he never said a word. Probably been reading it himself!
Bronagh:	They say it would have led to a revival of the Irish language if it had been translated into Gaelic!

Morag:	Can you remember what you used to wear to go out in?

*All the women improvise their fashion memories, including **Morag** who tells about her dad, a night-shift worker at the Steelworks, making her a hoop for under her petticoats in the fifties. It was completely rigid, so that when she went to sit down, it lifted up her skirts and showed everyone her underwear.*

Girls reappear, laughing and playing their ringtones and dancing.

Ellie:	Oh my god, I forgot my lunch money. Can one of youse lend me some?
Helen:	Sure, that's fine.
Abby:	Have you got that song - you know?
Caitlin:	Yeah I know it … no it's rubbish.
Elle:	I have it.
Abby:	Oh, send me it.
Elle:	OK.
Caitlin:	Yeah, but you have to love "Glee".
All girls:	*(Singing:)* Don't stop believing. *(They all laugh.)*
Caitlin:	Come on, there's the bus.

*They exit, followed by the **Women**, discussing their favourite music.*

Scene 3: Foreign Workers

SET: Bare stage as if in the street

*Enter **Katerina** and **Milica** discussing jobs.*

Background notes on Katerina and Milica

Katerina: "I came to Corby two years ago for love. I met a Corby man on the internet when I had been in England for one year. We are to be married next month. I was working as a carer in Wisbech. I left my family, friends, house and career at 47 to have an adventure, go the way of my heart and start a new life, following divorce from an abusive alcoholic husband.

I love it here. I love the language and my job at the school - I am a music teacher. Very few European people I know are lucky to be working in their profession. I help out at the Polish school on Saturday mornings. I only wish there were more clubs for the children. In Poland there is more. Here when the parents are working the children are stuck to the computer with no hobbies or interests.

And there is gang versus gang. I hear at the school how the English guys want to fight and even the girls have been beaten up for being different. That is such a shame. We have so much to learn from each other's cultures. I would like to start an international youth arts group. That way they will mix and grow and share together".

Milica:	"I am also coming here because of falling in love in 2005. I met a Croatian man from Corby on the internet and I married him here. Now we have two children. I miss my family back in Serbia, but I expected to marry and have a family and move somewhere, so I need to adjust to this new life. If you go on an adventure in a forest, you accept everything you see.
	But I find it very lonely here and boring … always housework and children every day. My husband is working all day. In Serbia I would have my family around me to help with the children. But here I am on my own.
	I like the way the children are learning here. It all seems equal. Everyone in uniform! In Serbia this one will have Nike on feet and this one, slippers. And here it is more posh. The kids are learning here to be diplomats from birth! Anyway, the queen is on the throne. My nieces always ask me "Auntie, auntie, did you see the Queen?" Like in the fairy stories! I don't want to break their dreams …
	People move now to Corby from many other countries. Some for love, like me. Some to study, but mostly to work. From Slovakia, Turkey, Germany, Estonia, Czech Republic, Zimbabwe.
	I wanted to be opera singer but instead I study landscape architecture, and now I am here with children."

Gaida enters SR and as she passes them, she knocks **Katerina's** handbag. **Milica** angrily responds in Serbian.

*Gaida apologises and asks where they are from. She starts a conversation with the women about life in Corby, how it was in Latvia, welcoming them to the town. **Gaida** asks if they are here looking for work and they say "yes" and then all turn to the audience.*

Katerina: *(Speaks in Polish, then says in English:)* Oh, but you don't understand … sorry. When I first came here, I wondered where I was because all I heard around me was Polish.

Milica: They always give the jobs to the Polish! When they hear I am Serbian they are not interested. Serbia is not in the EU.

Gaida: I don't suppose they will stay in the town. They are here for a job and then they will go back.

*They all say goodbye and **Gaida** leaves.*

***Milica** is rude about her being a boring old woman and the two younger women wander off after her.*

Scene 4: Lakelands Charity Shop

SET: Based on a community charity shop with a café area and tables, a book area, bric-a-brac, a few racks of second-hand clothes, a changing cubicle and a central till

MUSIC: MONEY - PINK FLOYD

Maggie and *Morag* enter and start setting out the shop.

Maggie is the head volunteer and bosses *Morag* around. Hierarchy is soon established: volunteer versus paid cleaner.

Enter *Karen*, Lakeland's fundraiser, who explains that today there is someone from Talking Books coming and that they should be set up in the book area. She gives *Maggie* leaflets, and sets herself up on her laptop out of the way in the book area with a Talking Books sign.

Maggie complains that she will not have time to tell her story, but what it would be if she could. Tells *Morag* about coming down from Scotland for the Steelworks with four children and a fifth on the way.

Meanwhile *Gaida* enters and rummages amongst the clothes, followed by *Milica* and *Katerina.*

Gaida: Why are you in here?

Milica: No job. We have to come here.

Katerina talks about always having had to wear hand-me-downs and also about looking twice in the mirror, based on this monologue:

"Every time I have some question about my body, how I have to wear, I wasn't scared to go to my mother and talk about it. And what she told to me is: 'Katerina, just be yourself and if you want to wear something just look in the mirror twice. And if you feel good and if you feel comfy, that's OK.'"

They decide to stay for a cuppa and go to the counter.

Maggie *is serving.*

Katerina:	What cake is this?
Maggie:	Ginger cake. It's home-made.
Katerina:	Can I have the recipe for it? I am trying to make a book of recipes from all the different countries here in Corby.
Maggie:	I'll ask my customers and keep them here for when you next come in.

Katerina, Gaida *and* ***Milica*** *go and sit down in the café.*

Meanwhile ***Linda*** *has entered and had a browse, and discusses wanting to become a volunteer with* ***Maggie****.* ***Maggie*** *thinks she means the hospice and launches into detail.* ***Linda*** *explains that she means the shop, now that she has free time since her daughter has left home.* ***Maggie*** *tells her to have a wander and watch a day at the shop.* ***Linda*** *sits ready to observe.*

Enter ***Catherine*** *bringing in a bag of her daughter Felicity's things. She asks about Talking Books.*

Maggie *calls* ***Morag*** *to deal with the bag.* ***Catherine*** *takes a cuppa over and joins* ***Linda.***

Maggie tells *Morag* she is going to hand out the leaflets, but stops as she sees *Patrice,* the Talking Books woman, arrive.

Patrice explains about the project. Her role is to interview people about their life stories, focusing on how they came to Corby. The interviews would eventually be transcribed and the recordings made available in the library.

Maggie starts to take her over to the book corner to set up, but is interrupted by *Karen* the fundraiser. *Maggie* self-importantly tries to introduce them, but the two professional women know each other from phone calls and are shaking hands, so *Maggie* is pushed out. She takes leaflets to the café.

Morag is serving when *Ada* comes in with books. She is a regular customer. She greets *Maggie* too. Browses books. *Karen* persuades *Gaida* to tell her story. *Katerina* goes with her.

Karen goes over to *Maggie* and *Morag* to discuss fashion show and shop sales etc. *Maggie* and *Karen* go to clothes rails.

Focus on *Linda* and *Catherine* who chat. *Catherine* is an English teacher with a new job. Daughter is leaving home and she is preparing a room for her granddaughter.

Gaida tells her story of coming to Corby - improvised but based on this monologue:

"The day we fled from the Russians was the last time I saw my favourite teddy. I was seven and a half. 'The Russians are coming', people said. So, like many others we decided to leave. We packed everything in wooden tea-chests. Winter clothes! All our precious belongings! But when the lorry arrived it was full of people and others were getting in. 'People only,' they said, 'and hurry!' I left my big teddy, the one I got for my fifth birthday, standing next to the piano with its paw on the keys. I was heartbroken!

All over the Baltic States, Latvians, Lithuanians, Estonians were fleeing from the Russian advance. Many on foot! In October 1944 we left on the last ship from the harbour. I don't know who was bombing us, but all the windows and everything glass on board was smashed with the noise and the blast. The town when we left was in flames. I didn't know where we were going. We landed in Poland. Polish families took us in. Me and my stepmother were there for four and a half months and spent most of the time in the cellar because there was nothing but bombing. That was a really bad time. Then we were put on goods trains, which took 15 days to get to Germany. I had my eighth birthday on that train.

When we first got to Germany, we got put in this school hall on straw mattresses. Me and my stepmother had one to share. She kept pulling the blanket over me. Was it to hide me or what? Being nosy, I peeked out the side and there was this bloke on the next mattress, haemorrhaging. He died there. It was horrible. And still the bombing! All the time bombing! The whole city! I don't know who was bombing us.

Eventually we were put in a United Nations camp. Displaced Persons' camps, they called them. Three, one after the other! We had to speak German because that was the language. With all the moves, we missed out on a lot of learning. When I came to England, my maths was more forward. Maths and art and things like that I could do. Anything that didn't need words. I didn't want to come to England, but I had no choice. We left my dad behind.

I came to Corby on my own in 1957 at 20, because I was ready for my own life. There were about 500 Latvians in Corby, my future husband amongst them. I knew of Corby from the regional Latvian Dance Group. I liked it well enough. We had a community, a church, Latvian school on Saturday morning and volleyball on a Sunday.

I had a feeling that maybe, finally, this displaced person had found her place at last!"

*When she mentions "Displaced person" that is the cue for **Katerina** to look at **Milica**. She interrupts, realising that there is a long story still to tell.*

Milica: Excuse me, I have to pick up my kids from nursery, so I like to tell my story now. Yours is very long. OK? *(To **Patrice:**)* My name is Milica. I came to Corby for love. I met my husband on the internet and now we have two children. I try to find jobs but no success. And that's my story.

Sorry, now you can carry on.
(She leaves.)

Everyone is a bit shocked at her rudeness.

***Gaida** resumes her story. Lights to focus on her.*

*Meanwhile **Katerina** wanders over to food counter and mimes talking to **Morag** about the food for her recipe book.*

*When **Gaida** finishes **Katerina** invites her to have food and they go and sit down together.*

***Catherine** stands ready to go and tell her story.*

*Meanwhile **Ada** has been eavesdropping.*

Ada: Can anyone tell their story?

*Realising that she has missed her turn, **Catherine** leaves.*

*Patrice welcomes **Ada**, who tells her story about coming to Corby based on the following monologue:*

"I came to Corby in 1975 to escape the violence at home. I'd grown up with it, but when my dad threw my new-born baby across the room, both me and my mum walked out. She wasn't prepared to see yet another generation be subjected to his violence, and I wasn't prepared to do his bidding and marry a childhood friend who was just out of jail in order to 'give my daughter a name'. I couldn't see what was wrong with my name!

So, there I was, 21 and homeless ... until my cousin in Corby called and asked me to look after his flat on Canada Square whilst he worked away on the oil rigs. We jumped at the chance. I wasn't eligible for a council house back home in Yorkshire, but in Corby, as a homeless mother, I was offered my own three-bedroom house above the shops on Welland Vale Road in no time at all. It was wonderful. I thought I'd died and gone to heaven.

It was refreshing to come to Corby. No-one judged me as a single mum. No name-calling here. No threats to take the baby away. Everyone accepted you for who you were. I was pregnant from a short-term affair in the army, but I wanted children and thought it would be OK to be a single working mum. Better than a loveless marriage, or a marriage of convenience.

We fitted right in. I always considered myself Aberdonian, having spent lots of time up there with my mother's family as a child. We used to have a clan gathering every two years, with relatives coming over from Canada and America. Corby was home from home."

*Enter **Alma**. She gives a bag to **Maggie** then browses books whilst **Ada** talks.*

*At the end **Ada** goes to the counter, orders food. General chat.*

*Ada goes to café and sits with **Linda**. **Morag** brings her food over and as she returns to the counter, the talking stops.*

*Ada takes her cuppa to the table and sits with **Linda**. **Karen** goes offstage.*

Linda:	I overheard you telling your story - you're so brave talking about what happened in our past.
Ada:	Why, what did I say?
Linda:	Well, you talked about the violence and abuse.
Ada:	Yes, there was plenty of that growing up. I never personally got hit. I was lucky. But it is hard watching your mum get beaten, and your sisters. You feel so helpless. I vowed I wouldn't put my kids through the same. So, I've kept my relationships with men away from them. I didn't want to risk exposing them to the sort of violence I'd seen.
Linda:	I grew up around that sort of thing too.
Ada:	Then tell your story. It could be good therapy to get it off your chest.
Linda:	I couldn't do that; I've never told anyone. I'm not ready for that.
Katerina:	Are you talking domestic violence? In Poland I know how to help women in that situation, but here I wouldn't know what to do.

Ada:	Well, I was a volunteer at Corby Women's Centre. They help women with all sorts of abuse. It's women supporting women in a safe place. There's also the Sunflower Centre for crisis situations, and a refuge in Corby for women and kids to escape violence.
Katerina:	When I wanted to leave my husband there was nowhere to go. And I didn't have enough confidence to do it anyway. It was only later I heard there was a safe house like this in Poland.
Linda:	Why did you want to leave?
Katerina:	He was an aggressive alcoholic. I was only 19 when I first got married - he was 23. First time he hit me was when I was pregnant with my daughter, and I put up with it for 23 years. So, in the end I divorced him.
Ada:	My mum and gran were both really strong women, but they both stayed for years and hid their abuse. They used to put on their coats, headscarves and lipstick and go out as if nothing was wrong, even though half the street lived the same way.
Linda:	People talk about the bruises, but there is the emotional abuse too.

Alma walks past **Patrice**.

Ada:	It's hard to get over both. It takes years to build up your confidence.
Linda:	And self-esteem.
Katerina:	It took me a long time to re-build my confidence, but now I'm doing what I want with my life.
Linda:	Yeah, I know how you feel. I even got a tattoo after I left him.

Katerina looks at her quizzically.

Patrice approaches Alma at the bric-a-brac, asking her to tell her story.

Patrice:	Where did you come from?

Alma explodes and says she is Corby born and bred. In her response she mentions all the foreigners, the displaced persons after WWII and the coming of all the Scots for the Steelworks. She also says that Corby people make things happen! This is improvised based on the following monologue:

"A lot o' folk might live in Corby, but they ent from Corby. I'm from proper Corby. Corby Village! I've always lived in the village. My folks 'ad a pub in the village. They wuh Weldonites, but there ent much difference. Weldon kids used to 'ave t' walk t' Corby village for some of th' lessons. But *they* wun't the outsiders! No! The real difference wuh Villagites an' Corby. Corby Village an' Corby didn't really get on well years ago. There wuz a mile between the Village an' the town. An' that wuh the divide. The Village guz as far as Oakley Road where the bridge is, 'alf-way down Weldon Road t' where the Sally Ann used to be, up over the railway bridge t' the Odeon, an' Cottingham Road t' the Conservative Club.

We kept ourselves to ourselves when the new 'uns arrived. Comin' in an' upsettin' the apple cart, bringin' things in and doin' things different and tryin' t' tek over. They couldn't understand us an' we couldn't understand them. They wuh sayin' things we didn't know and we wuh sayin' things they didn't know. Most of 'em came down from Scotland - Glasgow. They wuz what we called the 'evvy wuns. Couldn't understand a word they wuh sayin'! There wuz quite a few of them DPs from the Brigstock camp in th' village. See, one or two's alrigh'. But there wuz too many o' them others, too quick! Comin' 'ere, tekkin' over, with their foreign food an' all. Scotch bread, scotch pies!

Mind you, wherever y' wuz born we all ended up together in Rowlett School an' we 'ad t' get on. They'd come down from Stevie Way, up th' town centre an' around. A couple a bus load of 'em. They 'ad kids from the villages as well: Geddington, Gretton, Stanion, Brigstock.

Where wuz I born? Well actually born ... that wuz at the Brigstock camp, cuz they 'ad a maternity bit up there for if there wuz problems.
But I would never say I wuz from Brigstock. Corby Village, an' proud of it!"

Maggie and Morag are sorting stuff at the front of the display cabinet and get offended by what Alma says about Scots, but she goes on to say how good the Lakelands is and they are happy again. The foreign women think she is talking about them and are amused to hear she means the Scots were the foreigners. She leaves to go and sort out her dad, who has cancer.

Patrice sits and takes notes.

Gaida:	I'm sorry to hear about your troubles. I was very happy with my husband. We were happily married for 40 years.
Katerina:	I am happy now as a new wife. I came to Corby for love when I met my husband on the internet.

Linda:	My new partner is the nicest man you could wish to meet. We are really happy.
Ada:	My partner and I have been together for 13 years. She's Italian. We were made for each other.

At this casual referral to being in a Lesbian relationship, various levels of discomfort emerge, depending on how homophobic the characters are. Shock on some faces; slight moving away by some.

All improvise general chat as they move around the shop. Katerina moves to the books. Ada and Linda to clothes.

Enter Bronagh and Bernadette. Bronagh looks for an outfit, Bernadette goes to get a cuppa. Patrice invites her over. Morag brings her a cuppa. Background chat is now on silent so that Bernadette's story can be heard. Improvise based on the following monologue:

"It was 1959 when I first visited Corby. I stopped off for my younger brother's wedding on my way back home to Ireland from New York. Talk about round the world for a shortcut! Back home for Christmas, I learned that my elder brother and his intended decided to give Corby a go, what with the promise of so much work and all. But they needed a chaperone. A young woman going off with her man alone! And them not yet wed! She would have been the talk of the country!

So, I joined them and moved to Corby for good the next year. 22 years old, with my return ticket to New York in my pocket, just in case it didn't work out. Mary and I took digs together in York Road, whilst Sean found his own nearby. They were wed a month later and quickly got their own house. I got a job in a ribbon factory down St. Mark's Road and lived as part of a sizable Irish community up near St. Brendan's.

How did I find it? I remember the smell of the Steelworks. I'd washed New York out of my lungs with the good fresh air in Ireland. And the dirt! Having to wipe your washing-line three times before you could hang out the washing and even then, it'd come in with peg marks on. Living in a building site whilst the town was being built around you! I used to walk up Beanfield Avenue on my way to St. Brendan's, watching the new houses springing up and wondering if one of them would be mine one day. Sure enough, I ended up with number 114! I was always fascinated by new houses. On a Sunday when the men weren't working, I'd go round climbing in the windows of half-made houses and imagine them finished. Funny that. One of my sons turned out as a builder.

And the people … not as friendly as now I can tell you! Everyone was busy fighting their own corner. So many Scots intent on making it Little Scotland! And I couldn't understand a word they said. There would be a brood of Aberdonians cackling away in the factory in their own lingo and I would feel left out.

But my first Hogmanay put that right. I'd never seen anything like it. It was amazing. There was a full moon. The sky was full of stars. Frost on the ground, twinkling like diamonds. We went first-footing from house to house. Neeps and tatties and steak pie at Mrs McHagan's. Everyone's doors open … It was so warm and friendly. That was when I realised my plane ticket would probably never get used after all."

All *improvise general chat.*

Bernadette *goes to sit down at the table next to* *Gaida.*

Katerina *leaves.*

Meanwhile *Bronagh* *is trying things on in the changing rooms - a bare arm emerges as she throws clothes over the top.*

Patrice *is packing up.* *Karen* *sits with her. They leave together walking briskly, discussing how successful the day has been and the fact that* *Patrice* *needs to get to the library.*

Ada and *Linda* are still at the clothes rail. *Bronagh* asks for a lacy thing in front of them. *Ada* hands it to her and tells *Linda* the story of the see-through catsuit, improvised based on the following monologue:

"My biggest fashion hitch was my grandma's fault. Whoever said that generation was shy can think again. I was attending my sister's wedding and turned up in my army uniform as requested, since my cousin was going to be wearing his navy uniform. I had no time to shop for a reception outfit so I asked my mum to see to it. She sent my gran off shopping and she chose a white, lace, see-through catsuit. They were all the rage at the time. It wasn't until I was leaving the reception to go on to a nightclub that I realised how revealing it was. I literally stopped the traffic and a policeman asked me to go indoors quickly. From the stares of passing motorists to the fluorescent lights of the nightclub which, given my white underwear, ensured that I remained firmly in the public eye all night."

Ada exits.

Linda gets a form off *Maggie* and then leaves.

Scene 5: Shop Closing

*Maggie tells **Morag** to wipe the counter and goes over to sit with **Bernadette** for a cup of tea.*

Maggie: I see you told your story. I never got to tell mine. We've heard all sorts in here today. There was an old Latvian woman and a young Serbian woman, a Polish woman wanting recipes.

When I first came here it was mainly Scots and Irish … The odd DP … and even a few English!

Bernadette: *(Laughing in agreement:)* All these different nationalities … isn't it lovely?

And they are all here to make a better life for themselves, a job, and a house. That's what I did. There was no work in Ireland when I was young. That's why I went to America at 17.

Maggie: Most of us are migrants here in Corby.

Bernadette: That's what makes it so interesting. All the different cultures with their own ways, music, dance, food, clothing.

Maggie:	These European women are very stylish. They bring in some lovely clothes. Which reminds me, we are having a fundraising fashion show for the Hospice and we need models. Would you like to be one?
Bernadette:	When is it?
Morag:	*(Sitting down to join them:)* It's on the 25th at the Grampian.
Bernadette:	Yes, OK then.
Maggie:	I'll go and find the forms. *(Goes off to get forms.)*
Morag:	I haven't seen you for ages. Someone told me you got a divorce … is that right?
Bernadette:	It wasn't easy for me to make the break, being a Catholic and all, but I did the unthinkable. I left my husband and then divorced after a life sentence of 30 years. I got married again to another Catholic. This time I'm truly happy.

Maggie returns with the form and joins them as they are discussing Greenock.

Bronagh emerges with her choice of outfit and goes to pay at the counter. No-one is on the till, so she joins the group.

Maggie:	Well, I'm from Greenock and there really was a stigma. There is nothing wrong with Greenock folk.

Bernadette:	Well now we are all in the same boat. Tell anyone you are from Corby and you get the same reaction.
Maggie:	Well, this town is good to people. Did you hear that lass talking about the support she got coming here as a single mum?
Bronagh:	It is way better than being an unmarried mum in Ireland.

She tells the story of the County Homes, improvised but based on the following monologue:

"There was no law against having a boyfriend but you just didn't go too far, so to speak. Getting pregnant when you weren't married was a terrible offence and the punishment was great. You would be sent to a County Home and after raising your child for seven years, your child was then taken away from you. Children were sent to people who sometimes didn't look after them properly and had really hard lives. And the mother wasn't allowed to go home, she'd be sent to live elsewhere. I remember being in Longford and there were some of these young women and children playing in the yard and my mum pointed them out to me. It was a terrible thing to get pregnant, you'd rather be dead! It's been very hard for me to adjust over the past 40 years - things are so different now.

When I first came to Corby, some of the girls were talking about things that I didn't really know about and one of them said to me, 'Don't be acting all innocent, you were in America: you know all about this!' I was so offended I slapped her! If you'd been to America you were seen as a loose woman. But you couldn't have stayed there if you got pregnant, as there'd be no income to raise it and you didn't get the help you do today."

Morag:	It was like that in Scotland and no doubt here in England. Always about bringing shame on the family.

Bronagh: My mammy was a midwife - I don't know how that came about 'cos she'd never trained in the hospital or anything. All the children round and about were delivered by my mother, and if there were any complications she'd send for the doctor, but that seldom happened. You couldn't pick up the phone and call the doctor, you had to fetch someone to get their bike out and cycle three and a half miles into the nearest town for the doctor. In them days people had lots of children, so she was kept busy. Most of the children were born at night and I often didn't know she'd gone. When she'd go back the next day, I could go with her. One thing I hated was, "Who does he look like? Who *does* he look like?" and I'd think, "He looks like nothing on earth - just a scalded red face!"

(Coming back to the present:) Anyway, enough chat. I've this date to get ready for. Are you coming?

Bernadette: Yes. It's been a long day!

General chat.

Maggie: Shall I take for those?

Bronagh *and **Maggie** go to the till.*

Morag *collects the cups and puts them on the counter.*

Maggie *goes to get her coat. Then she checks round the* *shop.*

Maggie: *(To **Morag**:)* Don't forget these dishes, Morag. See you tomorrow.

*All go and leave **Morag** to clean. She talks to the audience as she does.*

Morag: My granddaughter said to me the other day, "Gran, I want to be buried with you! And if I die first, you have to be buried with me." What a thing to say! But see, I was that close with my gran too. I used to love going to Glasgow for a visit - she used to fuss me. I needed that. My own mum had too many kids and never had time for fussing us … Gran made me feel special. And I suppose, in my own way, I'm doing the same with Cathy. Her mum was poorly when she was a baby, so I looked after her a lot. That's what brought us close.

Sometimes when she comes to stay, she turns the telly off and asks to talk. "Let's talk, Gran," she says. "Tell me a story." And I do - like my mum told me. Mind you, she was a great storyteller. She loved nothing better than talking! I was only 21 when I realised I'd heard the last of her stories … and newlywed too! My husband took on a ready-made family - and somehow we coped. But then, I'd seen my gran. She'd had seventeen kids

- not all of them lived, mind! So, caring for a big brood is what I've seen, what I know.

It wasn't all hard work and no play though. Especially in the sixties when there was so much work around. You could walk out of a job you didn't like one day and have a new one the following week. And meeting all those other women put ideas in your head. We all had lots in common, but it got you thinking how things could be different. Who were they all? Ach, they'd come to Corby from all over. Just like today – all those different women – all with a story to tell.

She is tidying the rails. Enter granddaughter **Cathy**.

Cathy: Are you nearly ready, Gran?

Morag: I won't be long. Did I ever tell you, Cathy, one of my first jobs was in an underwear factory? I loved knickers! I used to have hundreds of pairs. We'd get them cheap, you see … I had them in all the colours of the rainbow. Lovely fabrics - frilly, lacy and often see-through!

Never had much money for fancy clothes, but I didn't care 'cos I knew what was underneath - lovely clean knickers! I'd change them two or three times a day. And I'd take great care of them. I used to dry them on the boiler so my brothers wouldn't see!

One time I was visiting my gran in Glasgow and she went to peg them on the line … I'll never forget her face! She was horrified! She wore seriously big pants and expected me to wear the same. Mind you, I feel the same about the bit of dental floss you wear nowadays!

Cathy: Gran! Honestly!
Can we go and buy shoes now?

Morag: I know your game, young lady! I used to try to get my gran to shop with me, 'cos I could wind her round my little finger! Whatever shoes I wanted, my mum would disagree. She always wanted the sensible ones and I wanted what was in fashion.

They leave together, locking up as they go.

ACT TWO

Scene 1: Bus Stop

Linda *enters alone and tells her story to the audience: being born in Corby, having her daughter and then escaping from a violent marriage. Improvised based on the following notes:*

Roots
"I was born in Corby in 1966, and I mean Corby! Not Kettering! The maternity unit. I grew up on the Exeter estate and then at 19 moved to Newcastle with my boyfriend for a couple of years. I insisted on holding the wedding in Corby, and soon after, we moved back permanently. You can go pretty much anywhere in Corby and you'll know somebody. Corby puts its arms around you.

Daughter
My Charlene's a fantastic kid and I'm so proud. She's pleasant ... she is not a type to go out every night of the week, she's never been a kid that's roamed the streets, and she is respectful of people. She'll stand and give it to me something chronic some days, but I know I can take her anywhere and not have to worry if she'll kick off. I can honestly put my hand on my heart and take credit for that. Because *I've* done that - on my own! She finished school this year and she's going to university. I was chuffed to bits, because I kept on saying to her from the age of 16, 'Don't end up how I've ended up, in a dead-end job'. She wants to do business. It makes me feel proud.

Patterns repeating
My mum was really young when she wanted to get married. Nineteen, I believe. And he was early thirties. So that was quite a big difference. Her granny basically told her: 'You marry him over my dead body'. Mum went ahead anyway and had quite a hard life with my dad. He battered her for twelve years. I must have witnessed it as a child but I blocked it in my memory. She chucked him out when I was eleven. Gran must have seen something that mum couldn't, staring her right in the face.

It's quite odd in a lot of ways. History has repeated itself with me. At nineteen I went against my own mum's advice and married an older man, and I've had a bad marriage. Not physical abuse, but mental.

Surviving an abusive marriage

We first met when I went to Newcastle with my friend. We started going out with each other long distance. I'd go up one weekend - he'd come down the next. Everything seemed fine until we started living together up there. I was very fiery to begin with. You know how you say to yourself, 'I'll never be like me mam!' Well, I used to shout, just like she did. That was my way of getting out my frustrations - shouting at him. For not one second did I think he would end up doing to me what he did. I used to think I was dead strong ... bolshy! I could take it or leave it. But they strip away everything you are. People say you don't see what's right in front of you. All the signs must have been there for me, too. Just like my mother before me.

Even though we were living in Newcastle we got married at St. Ninian's in Corby in 1987, so my friends and family could be there. I never really wanted to move away, but you know, in here *(indicates head:)* part of the brain is old-fashioned. 'I have to do what the man wants me to do.' Realistically, I should have stuck my feet in and went 'no'. It was a horrible experience. I hated it. I've always had my friends and my family and a job. I gave it all up. We lived together first 'cos I couldn't marry a man without knowing what he's like. If you come from a 'broken home', you need to be sure! I was really lonely for two years. I didn't work. I didn't know my way round. It was really quite frightening.

He had a small family, and I've always had a big family. His mum never had a friend pop in for a cup of tea, and I found that odd. Our house, growing up, there was always people in and out. We were very close-knit. Eventually, I managed to talk him into coming down to Corby, and I went back to work. We moved in with my mum and dad for a little while, which was a nightmare. They could see what I couldn't. I kept on thinking they were just being unfair. He's not the most sociable person, and we were a sociable family. He felt threatened by the closeness between me and my mum.

The minute Charlene was born is when it changed. It was very gradual. We were living on our own in a house on Kingswood by then. I decided ... we both decided, for me to stay at home till she went to school. I didn't see the point in having a baby, then giving it to someone else to look after while I went to work. It was a joint decision. He tried to keep me and our daughter in a little unit, and he didn't like any interaction into 'his' unit. As I said, I'd grown up with people coming in and out of my house. Part of me thought, 'I don't want that for my daughter, I want privacy.'

As Charlene got older, he started stripping everything away. He'd shout at me, and totally and utterly ridicule anything I tried to do. As time went on, I found I couldn't make a decision myself. I remember standing in Adams' clothes shop and I didn't know what to buy because I had him in the back of my head. 'Make sure it's the right size, make sure it fits, make sure it's practical.' I couldn't just go in and go 'That's pretty,' because he'd taken everything away from me. People say - how did you let it happen? Well, I didn't see it coming. I really honestly didn't see it coming.

I was trying very hard. If we had a family thing, he would never come. I would dread Christmas. My mum liked to see all her children, and because they didn't particularly get on, it was a nightmare. If I stood up to him? He made you feel like *you* were wrong. He never joined in events with my family, and he never did anything with *us* as a family. Just like my own childhood. I have no memories of doing things with my own dad … so it was quite a mirror.

I think I stayed in my marriage so long because I didn't want to be like my mum. I wanted to smash that mirror. The more I stuck my heels in the more damage I was doing to myself and Charlene. I didn't want her to be from a broken home. That is such a horrible term. Just 'cos you live with one parent doesn't mean it's broken. And it should be sole carer, not single parent!

Anyway, to work round her school times, job-wise, he did constant back shift and I done days. His usual trick was on a weekend. I dreaded weekends, because he would drink at home and I would go to bed so I didn't have to watch. The more he drank, the more he got cocky and full of himself, and the nastiness started verbally. I remember clear as anything, one Thursday I'd left the washing in the washing machine to hang out the next morning, and I'd forgotten to take it out the machine. He used to come home on a Friday night and put his work clothes in the washing machine, because I was never allowed to wash his clothes. I couldn't tell you why. He kept his pants and socks in a bag on the back of the store room door. I thought this was my fault because I wasn't good enough to wash his clothes. You should have heard him when he found the washer still full of wet washing.

His party trick was he could talk to you and not raise his voice and make you feel *that* size (*indicates tiny*), not shout and swear and show anger and emotion. Just the way he did it was very unnerving. To sit back now I can look at it objectively and say, 'That's not my fault', but at the time I couldn't.

When Charlene got a bit older, we'd always go round to my mum's on Christmas night. We'd stay a couple of hours, but I'd always be watching the time up here *(indicates head)* thinking, 'Am I being too long? I better go, I better go.' Instead of sitting relaxing for the evening thinking, 'I'm having a great time!' he was always in the back of my head.

Breaking free
How can you say you love someone if you batter them? It doesn't make sense to me. We split up in September, ripping our whole world apart. That first Christmas was a bit of a nightmare. Charlene was 13, we were coming home from my mum's in the next street and she said, 'Isn't this nice, we don't have to worry about coming back on time'. That's when I knew I had done the right thing.

From the minute Charlene was born he had like an inbuilt jealousy. Obviously, she'd felt that and must have heard what went on. Over the years when Charlene was growing up, I used to go into her bedroom and watch her sleep and think, 'I can't do this any more'. I knew I wanted to leave him but I couldn't - for her. And I didn't want to become a failure, another statistic. All I knew when I got married, was that I didn't want to end up a divorced person.

How did it happen? It was like a succession of events. I never opened his mail. He never opened mine. We had separate bank accounts. That's the way he wanted it and I just went along with it. It's a trust thing. To my cost I found out he'd been stashing money behind my back. I always worked - constantly. £10,000 behind my back, he'd hidden. So, what was he planning?

He paid all the bills, then if anything was needed for the house, furniture, whatever, it was halved between the two of us. If Charlene needed anything, rather than ask him for it, I always bought it. That's fair enough. But I never ever bought myself anything. I didn't have many clothes at all really! I bought a shirt once. It was orange and totally out of character for me. I always wore dark colours, never bright colours. And because it was so different, he asked me if I was having an affair. I worked and I was home, very rarely did I go out with the girls, so what time was there for an affair?

On that Tuesday I said 'I want you to leave.' He said, 'You can tell Charlene you're the one breaking up our family.' Typical him! Emotional blackmail! Control! He needs control of someone. He doesn't feel fulfilled unless he's in control. Charlene was at football, so when she came in, I sat her down and told her. Normal reaction! No 'I want you to stay together' or anything. The guilt I felt because I knew it was me splitting us up! I gave him till Sunday. Not for him - for her! Because I couldn't in my heart of hearts chuck him out there and then. He moved into Charlene's room and she moved in with me.

I wouldn't go home. I was like a hobo. I'd fell out with my mum at this time. She could see what he was doing and kept on telling me to get rid of him. So, I didn't have my mum when I needed her most in my life. Like I say, I was like a hobo. The girl next door to my mum's, we were friends, and if it hadn't been for her giving me the support, I'm not sure I could have done it. I would sit out on the path outside the front door because I couldn't face being there. In hindsight I should have said 'If you're going, go.' It would have been quicker, more painless. But I couldn't do it. At the end of the day, he's still her father.

That was the worst week of my life. I went through so many changes. I thought people could see through me. I felt I wasn't worth enough to be on the earth. It sounds a bit mental really. I thought I was abnormal because of the way I felt. It was quite an odd time. I went into like automatic pilot. Just did everything you need to do. So, did he go?

He went, with a bit of arguing, a bit of pushing. I woke up on the Wednesday morning to find him in the bedroom standing over me, which was quite a shock. He said, in that control-freak, quiet voice, 'It's a good job I am the person I am, because if not I'd have snapped your neck and took the consequences!' That was a bit scary, but I thought to myself, 'If I show him I'm scared now, that's it, I'm dead. '

Then it was the old 'You'll have to pay all the bills'. I was literally cacking my pants. 'How am I going to cope?' I'd never paid a bill in my life. That's how he'd wanted it. Whatever was inside of me, I took that phone upstairs and changed all the bills into my name, and thought, 'Up yours! Show fear now and I may as well be dead because my life won't be worth living!'

I must have been gathering strength as it was coming. On that last day, the Sunday, he stood on that doorstep and said 'I will give you every single penny I have in my bank if you let me stay.' What sort of person did he think I was? Did he think he could buy me? With my own money too!

We're still not divorced. It sounds a bit crazy, but he can still go for custody of Charlene till she's 18. I can't really take the chance, because he'd do it to me just to cause problems. I'm in no hurry to get re-married and she's 18 this year. After that he can't touch me. There's still that little bit of fear there. It never really leaves you.

Especially to begin with! Like I say, I went into auto-pilot and done what I thought I needed to do. We've got a dog and I was in the garden picking up its poo, and I'm starting to panic, thinking to myself 'He used to clear this up on a Sunday and I've left it till Tuesday'. I was in such a tight regime I couldn't allow anything to slide. Like Sunday dinner! If I went out the house without making Sunday dinner, there was a row. Or if I rushed back and made a Sunday dinner and the potatoes weren't quite boiled enough, there was a row. But now ... if I don't want to make a Sunday dinner, I don't! It feels like it's little things - but it's not. It's all about control.

Just after we split up was the best time of my life. I'd married at nineteen going on twenty and I'd never had a life. So, at thirty-eight I started enjoying myself. My first trip away on my own, I went to Ireland for a hen weekend with twenty girls and had a great time. On that trip I made the tiniest little rebellion and it felt great. I got three tattoos - that was my rebellion. I wouldn't have them on my arms or anywhere you can see them. I've got one on my foot and I think to myself, I can cover that with a shoe when I'm older. The sensible side's still there. But that tiniest little act of rebellion felt great. You see, without him in my life I can do that, I'm free to be me. Whoever that turns out to be!

Relationships
Patterns repeat. My mum married an older man at 19. My dad. He battered her for 12 years. She chucked him out when I was 11. I married an older man when I was 19. My husband mentally abused me for 18 years. I chucked him out when my daughter was 13. Same pattern! I hope she won't make the same mistake! Mind you, I am happy with my new partner - he's a lovely man. Once I get divorced, we may well get hitched, but I am in no hurry. Patterns again! My stepdad is a lovely man too. Everything you could want in a dad.

Cuddling
My mum's never been a cuddly, feely person. I don't know if it's her generation or how she was brought up, but when you think about it, it all slots in. Her own mum died when she was only three, and her father didn't want her. He was trying to put her up for adoption or put her into care. But her gran wouldn't let him and took her on as her own child, even though it reminded her every day of the daughter she'd lost. She hated my mum for that. So, I don't think they were very close.

My mum always said "I love youse" and when we were younger it was all cuddles. Personally, I don't think you should stop when you get to a certain age. Even at 18, Charlene will always have a cuddle, or she'll lay with me on my bed sometimes. I feel I have a bond with her and I know fine well it'll cripple me when she goes away. I've just been away for the weekend and I missed her terribly. She'll be off to college soon and the closer it's coming the harder it gets. I'm thinking 'Am I gonna cope?' Because, in a sense, she's half of me. Even all the time I was with him, Charlene and I always did everything together. Not as a family unit - just her and I.

Fashion

I honestly can't ever remember going shopping with my mum. Shoes or clothes! I never did it. We never had that sort of bond. It's only in the last ten to 15 years that I feel a connection with her at all. I always felt like I was on the outside looking in, because I had an older sister and they seemed to get on better than I did.

I rarely went shopping with my own daughter either, 'cos she was a real 'girlie' girl and I was never that bothered. My friend used to take her instead. There was the 'shopping for the prom dress' incident last year. I picked one out. 'That's a nice dress,'" I said to her and I put it on her. I wasn't quite sure which way it went. I thought it looked lovely, till the shop assistant said, 'I think you've put that on the wrong way.' What a brass! We were all laughing though. In the end my boyfriend picked one. It was a lovely black dress, gathered at the bust with wavy-like material and a knee-length, black, flat satin skirt.

We've got all the pressure now from magazines and models about how to look and what to show. I think my Charlene's an absolutely lovely girl - pretty and slim. But she's not the most confident person about her body. She thinks that she's ugly and fat."

Catherine enters and says she caught up with Talking Books up at the library.

Linda: What did you tell them about you, then?

Catherine improvises, based on the following monologue:

"I came to Corby in 1975 as a 31-year-old mother of two young children. My husband worked in the research department for British Steel. We were living in Rothwell and looking for a house to raise the family in. We wanted somewhere with a reasonable-sized garden and a fair amount of space. We had looked in the villages round about, but you either had to buy the old vicarage, which was quite out of our range, or settle for a new house on a tiny plot.

We never intended to live in Corby, but whilst house-hunting, we found these reasonably-priced, quite nicely-designed houses with a sense of space, right next to the prizewinning Kingswood estate. They were only a 15-minute walk from the school and the church, and we quickly realised that Corby offered us by far the best deal. We were beautifully situated next to Kingswood Nature Reserve and close enough to go for walks to Great Oakley. And people were much friendlier than in Rothwell! Even though I felt like the foreigner at times. So many people spoke in broad Scots, it seemed to me.

Though I'd left my full-time job teaching English to start a family, I was keen to carry on my career. So, I had a reciprocal childcare arrangement with a neighbour, which enabled me to teach part-time at the tech. And I still had the one weekly evening class. We kept up our existing friendships with my husband's colleagues and went sailing on Rutland Water. And of course, Edward cycling to work left *me* with the family car. So, although living in Corby was not our original intention, it served us very well indeed."

Gaida, Ada, Katerina, and Alma join bus queue and chat superficially.

Enter Girls SL, noisily talking about teachers they fancy.

Caitlin:	Is Cathy coming with us tonight?
Ellie:	Don't think so.
Caitlin:	Well, tell me on MSN later. There's my bus! *(She runs off.)*

Pursed lips from older women till the girls have left.

| **Linda:** | I raised my daughter on my own, but I have standards. |

Gaida:	Why are they so noisy? I thought they would knock me over and not notice.
Alma:	Children should be seen and not heard.
Catherine:	Well, I have a different view as a teacher, and a JP!
Ada:	Ah, they're just being kids.
Katerina:	These girls they show all of their bum. My grandmother told to me: Katerina, remember one thing. Never ever show any man all your bum. She's not talking about my bum exactly, but about never show what you are thinking, how you thinking, how you feeling, how you exactly are.

All exit for the bus except **Gaida.**

Gaida:	I think I will walk. *(Talking directly to the audience:)* My upbringing was really different. When I was 20, I traced my real mother - but I never met her. I didn't even know I was adopted till a few days before my 15th birthday.

Improvise the rest of the story based on the following notes:

"We were moving between lodgings again. I was going back and forth with the suitcase whilst my stepmother was at work. She couldn't afford to take the day off. I came across this big envelope, 'On His Majesty's Service', and I recognised it as what I had carried on the plane to England. Being nosy, I looked inside and there were the adoption papers.

Up until then my stepmother was the only mother I had ever known. When I asked her, she denied it and I got very confused. The papers were in Latvian - but my main language was German. My stepmother spoke Russian to her Ukrainian boyfriend and I hardly knew a word of English. I had forgotten how to put sentences together in Latvian. But I knew what I had read. She never confirmed it. And I memorised the details so I knew where my real mother lived.

A few years later, somebody I knew from dance practice was going to Latvia for a holiday. He told me he was going to the town where my real mother lived. He never saw her, but he found out from his family that she still lived there. I started to write to her. She wrote back to me, not too much. Every letter she wrote she said she was in agony with her joints and bones, so I've inherited that from her. But she never told me much about giving me away. I heard *that* story from my cousin.

As a girl, my mum was a maid and a servant for a lady. When she was pregnant with me her boss said she must choose. The job? Or her baby? When I was two days old, the lady took her to the station and watched her put me on the train. According to my cousin, my mum went to prison for six months for that, and then went back to work for the same lady until she retired. Somehow, I was found and taken to hospital, where I spent the first two years of my life. The children's specialist there had an aunt who wanted a child. She started coming to the hospital and taking me for weekends. I was in a children's home for the next three years. Then, when I was five, I got officially adopted by that family. The doctor ended up as my godmother.

I found out other details of my early years from the international certificate of inoculation which came with me when I left the children's home. It tells you birth details, how old I was when I started teething, sitting up, and walking. According to the papers I was already baptised when I was found. Originally, I was born a Catholic. When I got adopted my surname, my birthplace and my religion got changed. I can remember being christened as a Lutheran. I was five then. I can see myself sitting in the side room waiting for the christening and everybody fussing about."

Exit **Gaida.**

Scene 2: Girls' Home Life

MUSIC: To be chosen by girls

All girls on stage doing physical theatre piece with each sitting on the floor with a laptop and some food. Each has her own monologue revealing the reality of their life behind the façade.

All *exit.*

Scene 3: Back Home

MUSIC: SHE - ELVIS COSTELLO

The Women enter in same order as the start of the play and mime the end of their day. Girls enter in pyjamas and **Cathy** *is in a room with her gran* **Maggie***.*

One by one they move to the front, allowing the audience to ponder for a few moments on how varied all their lives are.

Join hands and bow, reflecting that they are all linked by being female.

CURTAIN

Heritage
by
Paula Boulton

Specially commissioned for and first performed as part of the Our Corby festival in 2011 at the Core Theatre.

Inspired by a picture in the Seaborne photo archive collection.

Synopsis

A local Corby woman takes her two granddaughters to visit the Heritage Centre to hand in some family history. They meet a group of re-enactors depicting Corby in 1911. The girls explore the War Memorial, a schoolroom and a typical cottage whilst meeting the notorious Lady Adeline from Deene Hall, the vicar's wife Mrs Clarke, and a pickaxe-wielding Cracker at the ironworks. During tea break we hear about the forthcoming Suffragettes exhibition and see the re-enactors let their hair down. The cleaner finds the place spooky after dark, and it is in fact haunted. We meet the ghosts of some of the characters from the opening scene and a Suffragette, who fill in their history for us. The ghosts go into hiding when a school choir arrive to practise, followed by a brass band. The piece begins and ends with a remembrance service and reminds us that "We remember, lest we forget".

Staging and Set

This was performed on a flat-floor stage with a set specifically made for the occasion. There was a life-sized replica of the War Memorial with all the names of the local fallen, a farm workers' cottage, a wheelbarrow and a pickaxe for the Ironworks, a coffin, a drawing-room area and a schoolroom of the period. The set was very lavish and spread out around the stage as separate exhibits. There was an old yoke, a milk churn and buckets centre stage to add a feel of the period. A small table with a gramophone on also placed the piece in time. Several listening stations were suggested with telephone handsets or earphones near each exhibit. At the back of the stage were four life-size portraits of the ghosts, painted on screens which could be rolled up or down. There was also a live string quartet, a recorder consort, a children's choir and a brass band.

Costumes and Props

Red and white poppies, mop, bucket, sweeping brush, desk phone, books, photos, laptop, bag, tea-trolley, mugs, teapot, gramophone record.

All the re-enactors were dressed according to character, with Lady Adeline in particular in splendid evening dress of the period and wig. The Suffragette was dressed in prison clothes. The modern-day characters wore normal clothes.

Projection

The Seaborne archive photos are projected on a loop throughout.

Characters in Order of Appearance

WMW: the women at the War Memorial

Rosy: A visiting grandmother

Steph and **Sally:** Rosy's granddaughters

Brenda: The archivist

Schoolmarm/Tracy: 1911 Schoolmistress

Cracker/Sheila: A worker in the Ironworks, 1911

Farm worker/Bridie: Irish woman in 1911, living in a traditional cottage

Mrs Clarke/Maggie: The Vicar's wife in 1911, well-to-do

Lady A/Anna: Lady Adeline from Deene Hall, who is in real life a choir teacher and Polish

Student: studying about the Suffragettes

Betty: the cleaner

Two men: optional extra. Two men sitting next to a gramophone as if in a photograph of the era. Scene shifters

Ghosts: Lady A, Suffragette, Schoolmarm, Farm Worker: These can be played by the original re-enactors, or other cast members.

Intro

To set the atmosphere, the visual script of old photos from the Seaborne collection is projected onto a screen to suggest the 1900s. Two men sit either side of a gramophone mimicking one of the photos.

MUSIC: SELECTION OF CLASSICAL MUSIC - LIVE STRING QUARTET

Scene 1: Memorial 1

This scene happens either in front of the curtain or with the main stage in darkness.

Cast *enter chatting casually. Each woman gets three poppies from* ***War Memorial Woman***. ***Fliss*** *has four. They spread out across the stage. The sound of 11 o'clock strikes.* ***Cast*** *say the names of Corby men who died in WWI, and each time throw a red poppy as if onto the memorial.*

Fliss: Fred Marshall.

MUSIC: THE LAST POST, performed live by a single bugler if available.

War Memorial Woman *comes forward as the others exit chatting through door SR; they go backstage and take their places on set behind curtain.*

NB. This piece can be delivered in a spotlight if there is no curtain.

WMW: Each flower a life, each life a name
Each name a man, with family, friends and neighbours
A man who once lived and loved and breathed this air
And walked the streets of Corby.
But how true is our memory?
We use memorabilia to visit yesteryear
Photos, books, the internet, and objects we hold dear
Official dusty documents all have their part to play
To reconstruct a life that's gone and ponder at its ways.
Diaries tell it how it was - your mind fills in the blanks.
There are stories told by word of mouth
So pass them on with thanks.
For when 100 years from now someone looks back and asks
Your heritage is what they'll find. Are we up to the task?

Scene 2: Intro to Heritage Centre

Curtains open to reveal Heritage Centre. The women are in costume and are spread around the stage in various mini-sets depicting various parts of our history. An Ironworks, a drawing-room, a farm, a school. A soundscape of noises, from the Ironworks, of a pick axe breaking rocks, farm noises, school playground etc. helps set the scene.

It is important to let the scene run long enough for the audience to have a good look at each exhibit before moving to Scene 3. If it is possible to stage this immersively then this would be the chance for the audience to actually "visit" the centre.

Scene 3: Arrival of Visitors

Brenda enters FSR, puts her laptop and bag down on desk, followed by visitors Rosy and her two grandchildren Sally and Steph.

Sally: This is not the town centre! It's the old village!

Rosy: I said we'd go up town when I've finished here.

Steph: Come on! It won't take long! Think about it, if we do what nana wants, we get new shoes!

Rosy: *(To Brenda:)* Excuse me. I've got some information about my husband's family, the Marshalls. Corby born and bred. He's been re searching their background and thought it might be of use.

Brenda: I'd love to talk to you but I just need to get t things set up first. There's plenty to see in the main hall, or the café is open if you want to get a coffee.

All exit through door DSL.

Scene 4: Schoolgirls and Mrs Clarke

*Re-enactors start talking – an optional opening soundscape to create atmosphere. **Brenda** enters the main room. **Brenda** talks to all the women in turn about the next exhibition. **Sally** and **Steph** enter nervously and go and play in schoolroom. **Schoolmarm** strikes up a conversation with them.*

Schoolmarm: Can you imagine what school was like 100 years ago?

Sally: Clearly, they didn't have interactive white boards. Did they?

Schoolmarm: That's true. They used to write on slates which were hung around the kids' necks in case they dropped them. It was really crowded, sharing two to a desk in a class of 46 or sitting on benches at the back. In the nursery there were 36 babies crammed into a room made for 24, looked after by an unqualified monitoress. Boys and girls in separate rooms. Water running down the walls. It sounds like the sort of school kids in the third world cope with. Really unhealthy.

Sally: What, like those Oxfam pictures?

Schoolmarm: Something like that.

Sally: Why was it so bad?

Schoolmarm:	Well, it had been built for fewer children when Corby was smaller. The problem was: there was really poor sanitation in the village and that, combined with overcrowding, meant that there were continuous outbreaks of infectious diseases amongst the kids.
Sally:	What, like swine 'flu? Measles?
Schoolmarm:	Yes, measles. If we look at this school logbook it shows a time when three-quarters of the kids were absent with measles. Some even died!
Sally:	Deaths from measles? Where does it say that?
Schoolmarm:	Right there. *(Points.)*
Sally:	*(Reading:)* 6th March 1909: from 9th Feb to 3rd March there occurred eight deaths from Measles.
Schoolmarm:	Some got bronchitis and pneumonia as well.
Steph:	*(Reading another doc:)* Ringworm, Chicken Pox, Whooping Cough, Influen za, Scarlet fever, Meningitis.
Sally:	Meningitis? My friend nearly died of that last year.

Schoolmarm: It was really hard to stop the infections spreading. Can you imagine hanging sheets soaked in disinfectant between people to stop the germs?

Steph: Did it work?

Schoolmarm: There was no treatment. Children died from diphtheria as well. It took six years and lots of deaths before they finally pulled the school down in 1915.

Steph: Why did it get so overcrowded?

Schoolmarm: Bit like now. In 1881 there were only 758 people in Corby. By 1911 that number had doubled. Now how many is that?

Steph: *(Picks up chalk and does a sum on the blackboard:)* 1516.

Sally: How do you know there were that many people? Is that like from the census and stuff?

Mrs Clarke: *(Has been nosing in on the conversation - picks up her diary)* And diaries! Come and look at this. It's a diary that Jessica Clarke, that's me, the Vicar's wife, kept. *(She reads a passage, indicating it to the children:)* "Building is going on rapidly in the village, nearly 40 new homes have been recently erected and many others in contemplation."

Steph: Aren't we doubling our population again at the moment?

Schoolmarm: Yes. And then - just like now, local services were bursting at the seams whilst they caught up - because they weren't ready for such a rise in the population.

Sally: Why did people first come to Corby?

*Enter **Lady A**, late for work. She is met by **Brenda** who scolds her and they uncover the coffin together.*

Mrs Clarke: People came here for jobs. Originally the majority of Corby families were in hand-loom weaving. The industry collapsed in 1850 and everyone was out of work. There was real poverty and no prospects of anything else.

Steph: Sounds like when the Steelworks closed in the eighties.

Mrs Clarke: It was only when the railway was built that things began looking up. Making bricks for the tunnel brought more people in and then they discovered the iron ore, and that led to blast furnaces being built and of course more workers were needed. You can listen or read about it here. This exhibit has diary extracts from around 100 years ago.

Jessica Clarke's one, and the Reverend Bartlett. *(Hands her the phone - both visitor and Sally listen to it together.)*

Rev Bartlett *(Pre-recorded voice. Posh accent:)* "Sited at Corby were fifty huts that housed the Navvies. Each hut contained seven men; some men were accompanied by women with children under sixteen years of age. In addition to the huts was a Shanty Township and some of the men lodged in the village."

Sally: Didn't Granddad live in huts when he first came to Corby?

Steph: That's right. Brigstock camp in the thirties. *(Sits in chair.)*

Sally: He came for the Steelworks. He told us about other men in digs sharing the same bed on alternate shifts. That's what foreigners do now.

Mrs Clarke: Funny how history repeats itself.

Sally: What you just told us about the new schools and illness -
it's the same now too.

Schoolmarm: How do you mean?

Sally: Well, we've had lots of new schools opening recently. They are pulling down the old ones. And we had an outbreak of TB at our school last year.

Schoolmarm: You're right there. My son got it. Apparently, Corby's always been a TB hotspot.

Mrs Clarke: That's true. My aunt used to work at the sanatorium in Rothwell where the TB patients went.

Steph: Corby's always in the paper 'cos of its poor health profile. Sounds like that has not changed much either.

Mrs Clarke: No, but at least we have decent sewage now. There was a battle to get that sorted. There are records of the enquiry. My husband, Rev Clarke, was on the panel. A Mr Langley thought we didn't need proper sewers. Because, as he put it, "95% of the population are of the labouring class."

Schoolmarm: Yes, they recommended we continue to use what they called "the pail method".

Sally: What, shit in a bucket? EEEUW! Gross!

Schoolmarm: Anyway … *(To child:)* that doesn't tell *you* anything about what school was like.

Sally: What subjects did they do?

Schoolmarm:	The head teacher was really keen on history, music, and drama. There was more emphasis on domestic subjects for girls to prepare them for service or running the home.
Steph:	But what if they wanted to go to college?
Schoolmarm:	Women weren't allowed to do degrees. Different expectations nowadays. Look at these. *(Holds up various items of clothing:)* This is what they made in needlework and then sold to raise money for the school. *(Girls rummage)*
Mrs Clarke:	I was still making things like that in the 1940s.
Steph:	*(**Sally** reads out a label saying 1s 6d. **Steph** corrects her:)* That's old money, "one shilling and sixpence".

Sally puts on knickers. *Cracker* goes over to books.

Steph:	Isn't that child labour!
Sally:	Yeah! If those kids were alive now, they'd make clothes for Primarni.
Schoolmarm:	Most children in the "labouring classes" left at 14. The boys went into the farm, fields or furnaces. And the girls went into service, until they got married.

*(**Rosy** and **Brenda** exit)*

Sally: That changed during the world war though, didn't it? Women had to do the men's jobs while they were away. I saw an exhibition at the Imperial War Museum.

Schoolmarm: The exhibit over there is all about what women in Corby did during the war.

Steph: That looks fun - *(To **Sally**, indicating knickerbockers:)* Get them off and we'll have a look.

Scene 5: Archivist and Rosy

Brenda and Rosy enter SL chatting, carrying coffee, and settle at the desk.

Brenda: Right - let's see what you've got.

Rosy: This is the family tree. And I've got some photos. *(Pointing:)* That's the gamekeeper's cottage on the Deene Park estate where his great granddad lived.

Brenda: There's one like that opposite the boating lake - apparently 12 people lived in that tiny house.

Rosy: This is Fred Marshall junior who was killed in the First World War. His name is on the War Memorial. This is a picture of the Lloyds "black houses", as they were called, where his granddad lived. Built for the ironstone workers. Notoriously damp. And then I've got this newspaper clipping from when his granddad died in 1955. He helped to build the first furnace for Lloyds and drove the first engine at Stewarts and Lloyds. And he was in the Corby Silver Band.

Brenda: It's really interesting. Can I keep these? I wish more people would do this. We need to collect people's stories before they take them to the grave.

Rosy: Anyway - I better go and fetch my granddaughters - we've got some serious shopping to do!

Brenda: We're trying to encourage more young people to come in - get them to bring their friends down.

Rosy exits.

Scene 6: Cracker, War Memory, Coffin

*Farm woman goes over to **WMW**. The girls are trying out the pickaxe and shovel. **Cracker** sees them and hurries back.*

Cracker: Steady on - that's real - you could hurt yourself! *(Retrieves pickaxe:)* Let me explain what all of this is. Around here women's war work was in the Ironworks. Crackers, we were called. Used to have to break up the slag with pickaxes and load the stones onto rail trucks. We worked alongside the POWs from the detention centre.

Sally: How come there were prisoners if there wasn't any fighting here?

Steph: Any Germans in the area would have been locked up and kept in a camp, just for being German. They were considered the enemy even if they weren't fighting, Sally!

Cracker: Crazy thing was that some of their younger brothers had been born here in Corby, so they had been conscripted and were off fighting with the Northamptonshire regiment against their own relatives. One woman, Mrs Villette, made friends with the prisoners. She managed to smuggle them in tobacco.

It really annoyed the top brass when they found out. We were all suddenly meant to hate people we'd grown up with, just 'cos they came from Germany.

Farm Woman wanders over to Cracker to get the girls to come to her.

Cracker: There were Czech soldiers stationed here too. It seems there have always been eastern Europeans in these parts.

Sally: *(Wandering off to the cottage:)* So this coming here from other countries thing isn't new? A hundred years ago there were people from all over, just like now?

Cracker: Yes.

Farm woman: Yes ... people have always travelled for work. Corby men used to follow the harvest - which even took them over to Ireland. *(Takes Sally to cottage.)*

Steph: *(To Cracker:)* But not everyone is from somewhere else! Some families go way back. We're one of the old Corby families - the Marshalls. Our great-granddad married into the Dixons, another old family. I saw the family tree my nanas brought in. Then there were the Spriggs - three of the girls in that family married three of the Marshalls. One of them got killed in the war.

WMW: *(Calling **Steph** over:)* There is a Fred Marshall on the War Memorial.

Steph: That'll be our great uncle - Sally!
(Girls explore the war memorial.)

WMW: *(To **Sally**:)* There is a story of one lad, not much older than you. Came home on leave. Had a rest. Caught up with his family. But the thought of going back to the trenches was just too much for him. He threw himself off the train that was taking him back to France.

Sally: Oh my God!

WMW: And those who did come back were maimed, disabled or left to fend for their relatives. Like the bugler in the Fourth Northamptonshire Regiment. He fainted during the opening of the War Memorial. But rather than me tell you the story, there is a diary extract about it. Listen!
*(Hands her the phone - **Sally** and **Steph** listen.)*

Mrs Clarke *(Pre-recorded voice. Posh accent:)* "At the close of the service ceremony, just as the buglers had sounded the Last Post, one of them fainted, overcome with emotion. We were glad to get him to the rectory where after somewhat recovering he told us he was the last of seven brothers who had served in the Army and had sounded the Last Post for them all and had been wounded twice himself. The solemn service had upset him very much. Now he had to look after the widows and children of them all."

Steph: *(Playing with wool:)* I'm gonna find Nana - I reckon she'd like to see this.

Sally: Right, I'll just look round.
*(**Lady A** sits up. **Sally** wanders to coffin and asks **Lady A**:)* Who are you and why are you in a coffin?

Lady A: Who am I? I am Lady Adeline, the Countess of Cardigan from Deene Hall. My favourite party game was to try my coffin. Happy memories!
How do I look?

Sally: Weird!

Lady A: *(Climbs out:)* I also loved sketching - shall I do your portrait?

Sally: No, thanks!

Lady A: I lived to be 91. I used to visit Corby a lot to help the poor people. Of course, we had servants from here. Maybe your great-grandparents worked for me.
*(Helps **Sally** get in the coffin.)*

*The other **Women** protest. Enter **Steph** and **Rosy** intending to show her nana the war memorial. They see **Sally**.*

Rosy: What on earth are you doing?
Get out of there. Show some respect!

Sally: It's great fun here, can we come again?
I had a go in a coffin and got to dress up.

Steph: Shall we go up town now then?

Rosy: I don't know -
I can't leave you two alone for a minute!

The girls start protesting.

Sally: But you said!

Steph: Why do you always have to spoil it?

Scene 7: Student and Archivist

Brenda is sweeping up poppies.

Student: Excuse me, I wonder if you can help me, I'm researching women around the time of the First World War, and I wondered if you have any local information?

Brenda: You're in luck! This is the last day of our "Corby Women 100 years ago" exhibition. *(Goes to desk to get leaflet.)*

Student: Excellent.

Brenda: And as it happens, we know quite a lot. There were a couple of notorious characters in the area. *(Looking for a photo:)* One woman refused to pay her tax, saying if she wasn't good enough to vote, then why should she pay tax!

Student: *(Engrossed in leaflet:)*
That's the sort of thing.

Brenda: If I were you, I would talk to Sheila in the main room. She's the one with a pickaxe!

Student: Pickaxe?

Brenda: We have various people in there dressed as they would have been one hundred years ago with artefacts and historical archive material. They just help to bring it alive. Sheila is one of the Crackers, the women who worked in the Ironworks in the First World War. Through the café.

The phone starts to ring. **Brenda** *indicates door as she turns to answer the phone. Enter* **Rosy** *and* **Girls** *through door.* **Student** *heads off in the direction she indicates, passing others on her way out.*

Brenda: Hello, Corby Heritage Centre. Yes, we are always looking for volunteers … Great, a social history graduate would be more than welcome … Fine, any time from ten till four … OK … Look forward to meeting you. *(Finishes sweeping up and goes off.)*

Scene 8: Tea Break

Betty arrives with the tea-trolley. The Women gather round to get tea. They take off wigs, put down shovels and generally loosen up.

Anna: (*Entering grandly:*) I am sick of getting in and out of that coffin.

Maggie: I would have been happy to oblige!

Betty: If the coffin had been wider!

Anna: (*Continuing uninterrupted:*) That woman was crazy.

Maggie: You're telling me. According to her memoirs, she held what was probably the first ever car-boot sale.

Anna: What do you mean?

Maggie: Well, she was destitute at one point, so she spread all her dresses on the grass and invited folk up to Deene Hall to buy them.

Anna: Seedy parties, car boot sales ...

Maggie: (*Interrupting whilst pushing the tea-trolley around like a bike:*) And she rode around on a bike in knickerbockers!

Sheila:	All right for her kind. She never lifted a finger in her life. She was a lady of leisure. I bet she couldn't have lifted a pickaxe. *(Picks it up and swings it menacingly as she speaks:)* This is like weight training and anger management therapy all in one. Every time someone pisses me off, I imagine it's their head on the block! *(Hits shovel inside wheelbarrow.)*
Tracy:	My nana lived in a stately home just like Deene Hall.
Carol:	Are you posh then?
Tracy:	No. She was a scullery maid. She said the Lord of the Manor had a roving eye!
Bridie:	That's an understatement! You might have noble blood in your veins.
Tracy:	What do you mean?
Bridie:	He had his pick of any of the serving girls and it was common practice to "deflower" them the night before they wed!
Sheila:	Deflower! There's a euphemism if ever I heard one. You mean rape. It's disgusting. No wonder women were militant.

Betty: I heard one woman saying her granny was a Cracker when she was younger. I nearly said "so was I"!

Sheila: Anyway. Let's have a sing through the Suffragette song ready for next week's exhibition. *(She stands at the front and conducts. The rest join in singing low and unrhythmically)*

MUSIC: NANA WAS A SUFFRAGETTE - JULES GIBB

Anna: *(Interrupting:)* Why is it so low? *(Sings gruffly:)* "Nana was a suffragette." We are women and I am a soprano. Let's try it higher. *(Sings as operatic soprano:)* "Nana was a suffragette!"

Bridie: You'd frighten the cows, squawking like that! *(Goes and sits down.)*

Sheila: You try! (**Anna** and **Sheila** swap places.)

All: *(Singing high:)*
"Nana was a suffragette - over 95."

Betty: *(Coming forward enthusiastically:)*
Let's jazz it up a bit like Sister Act. A bit of rhythm.

All: *(Singing enthusiastically and dancing unaware of Brenda arriving)*

Brenda: What on earth is all this noise about?

All: *(Improvised response e.g.)*
We're practising for next week.

Brenda: *(Looking disbelieving:)* May I remind you - we are still open to visitors even if it is the afternoon lull and your tea break? I do expect a certain amount of decorum from my re-enactors. Anyone walking in on this wouldn't know what to make of it. Back to your places.

*The **Women**, chastened or defiant, in character get back to their areas.*

MUSIC: NANA WAS A SUFFRAGETTE - JULES GIBB

Scene 9: Student and Cracker

*Student enters SL and approaches the **Cracker**.*

Student: Are you Sheila?

Cracker: That's me.

Student: I recognized you by the pickaxe!

Cracker: What can I do for you?

Student: I was hoping you might have the local angle on women in WWI. I've just started my dissertation.

Cracker: Sounds interesting. What made you choose WWI?

Student: Well - I was on the anti-cuts demo recently in London.

Cracker: So was I.

Mrs Clarke: Ah! That was you breaking windows was it - with your pickaxe?

Cracker: I was in the peaceful part of the demo.

Student: As were most of us. Anyway, I saw a statue - right there near the war memorial - about all the women who worked during the 2nd World War. And I realised that no-one seems to talk about women in WWI.

Cracker:	Well, locally many women worked in the Ironworks. That's what all this is. We broke up the slag with pickaxes and loaded it onto carts. Heavy, dirty work. They called us the Crackers! These would go to the railway sidings - where other women would load the wagons - all done by hand. Not all of the men had gone to war of course. Like in WWII, keeping the Ironworks going - that was a reserved occupation. Other women were working in the furnaces alongside the men in the fitting gangs.
Student:	Any pictures?
Cracker:	There's the one of the Crackers that my character is based on, but you get a better idea of what the work entailed from Peter Hill's books - "Images of England" and "Corby at War". There's a copy over here. *(Heads off to books:)* Come on, I'll show you.
Farm Worker:	We had to keep the farms going, of course.
Schoolmarm:	Yes, and also nursing. There is evidence in the tunnels under the old Steelworks of activity from the First World War, so women were bound to have been involved with nursing returning soldiers.

Student:	It's amazing to think that women were so crucial to the war effort but still didn't have the right to vote!
WMW:	The next exhibition is about the Suffragettes.
Student:	Who was there round here?
Mrs Clarke:	Well, in this area there was a very well-known working-class Suffragette called Alice Hawkins. And we know that Corby women were involved, because one woman talked about going out to meetings with a brolly in her bag in case the police got heavy with them.
Student:	Nothing's changed there then! Is there any info on her?
Mrs Clarke:	She organised the women of Kettering into a Trade Union for women shoe workers, and apparently Sylvia Pankhurst drew a picture of her.
Cracker:	Shame we didn't have anyone here doing the same. The conditions in the Ironworks were appalling. Mind you, the men soon put a stop to that. They were on strike even before the second blast furnace opened back in 1911, over the right to join a union.

Student:	Anything more on Alice or the Suffragettes?
Schoolmarm:	The ET did an article about her recently to launch the YouTube piece her grandson's done. It's called "Boots, Shoes and Suffragettes".
Student:	Was that Alice Hawkins? I heard them talking about it on the Jeremy Vine show the other week. They were discussing how we romanticise the Suffragettes nowadays, but treated them appallingly at the time.
WMW:	It's always like that though, if you dare to speak out. But that's how change happens. It's the history of protest.
Student:	Look at Nelson Mandela - 27 years locked up in jail, breaking rocks like Aileen - and then released as a hero to become president of South Africa.
WMW:	And the women of Greenham Common were portrayed as troublemakers and vandals in the eighties, but 25 years on, it's "the brave women of Greenham Common"!

Scene 10:
Farm Woman and Group Discussion

Farm Woman: Come and sit with me awhile.

Student goes into cottage area and sits on a stool where she joins in with wool winding.

Farm Woman: You couldn't have been a protester or Suffragette without someone to mind your kids! Too many women were busy trying to stay alive. They had no time for new-fangled thinking. And there was no way you would have survived without poaching. A rabbit or a hare on the back of the door would have been a common sight. And not just here, wherever labourers lived.

Student: What was farm work like?

Farm Woman: The conditions were terrible. Low wages, not enough to live on. Farm workers would go gleaning.

Student: Gleaning?

Farm Worker: Picking up the left-over ears of corn to make bread. Just like on the slag heaps, scrattin' for coal.

Cracker: The farmers round here were against it by all accounts. Thought the farm workers left too much behind on purpose.

Farm Woman: Most people would have had a pig or a chicken and a veg patch to grow their own food. Much healthier than now.

WMW: There are folk going back to those ways again. Practising for when the oil runs out.

Farm Woman: We had no ovens in them days; you used to have to take the joint down to the pub on a Sunday.

*Schoolmarm, **Lady A** and **Mrs Clarke** exchange a look, joking about a joint of beef.*

Farm Woman: There's a story of one lad who dropped it one day on the way back. A whole joint of beef rolling down the bank. I bet he got a clip round the ear when he got home.

Student: All very interesting. I need to be off now. *(She leaves.)*

Farm Woman: *(Calling after her:)* I could show you how a hay oven worked.

Student: That'd be great. *(Exchanges a look with **Cracker**:)* I'll be in touch.

Cracker:	*(Sarcastically:)* Scintillating stuff.
Farm Woman:	You'll be glad of it soon enough, what with energy prices going up and all.
Mrs Clarke:	I used to teach the Guides about hay ovens.
Lady A:	*(Sitting up:)* In Poland we cook rice in the bed! (**Women** *look confused.*) Wrap the quilt around the pot and leave it to cook itself.
Cracker:	Now you come to mention it, they did something like that when I lived in Germany. Rice pudding, wrapped in blankets, left to cook itself.
Farm woman:	I rest my case!
Cracker:	Bring it on, British Gas!
Brenda:	*(Enters carrying Suffragette sashes and places them in wheelbarrow:)* OK folks. That's the end of Corby one hundred years ago. Don't forget to come in early on Monday for a run-through of the Suffragette exhibition. *(She goes back to her desk.)*

*Now that it is 5 o'clock, the **Women** all leave and the centre shuts. We see them walking away in normal clothes.*

Lady A:	*(Struggling to get out of her coffin:)* Can someone help me!
Cracker:	*(Walking past with her pickaxe and brandishing it:)* What sort of help?

Mrs Clarke and *WMW* go over and pull her out. They natter and leave.

Scene 11: Cleaner and Archivist

Archivist gets men to move the gramophone into the main room. The Women chat as they work and the men leave by the back door. Meanwhile, Betty enters and starts mopping and cleaning.

Anna: *(Entering without her wig. To Betty:)* I'll be back later with my choir.

Betty: OK, I'll leave the door open.

Brenda: Don't worry about cleaning up ... we'll make a mess taking all this down. Give us a hand! *(They cover up coffin and chat.)*

Betty: I'll be glad to see the back of this. Anyone would think there'd been a murder!

Brenda: You know, I was told Corby was full of Scots but you're the only one I know.

Betty: Well, it's changed recently. It's not little Scotland any more, lots of newcomers, just like we were.

Brenda: And I was told that it was a hard town, whereas everyone seems really friendly?

Betty:	That got blamed on the Scots. But I read in one of these books - where is it, "The Foundation of a Steel Town"? - that to be a member of the Corby gang 100 years ago, you used to have to be willing to defend yourself with a five-foot ash pole. So, Corby folk have always known how to stand up for themselves.
Brenda:	Did your family come here for the Steelworks?

She settles down in one of the chairs.

Betty:	Yes, my dad walked here in the thirties.
Brenda:	Walked?
Betty:	Yes - he walked down from Glasgow. *(She wanders around and tidies as she talks:)* They blame industrial militancy on the Scots too. But that's not Scots, it's workers. It says in there about a big strike back in 1911 at the new blast furnace. Over the right to join a union. Mind you, depends which side you are on. As always. *(**Brenda** is really interested.)* The men tell it as a struggle for better pay and conditions. How they formed a union and then got told by Mr. Lloyd that they had to choose. The union or their job. *(Picks up diary:)* The Vicar's wife saw it differently. There's always been a split though. Us and them. *(Slams down*

diary.) But where would the world be without us labourers? The weavers, the navvies, the brickies, the Ironworkers, the Steelworkers, and us cleaners. The people that build the world that the rich folk rule.

*She goes to the photos at the back and rolls up the **Lady A**, **Suffragette**, **Schoolmarm** and **Farm Worker** photos, leaving four picture frames empty. Then she goes to her mop.*

Brenda: Would you mind telling me that again so I can record you? I want to try putting people's stories on the "Our Corby" website.

Betty: Time and a half?

Brenda: That's not up to me, I'm afraid.

Betty: OK, I'll give it a go.

Brenda: Put your mop down then.
I've got a dictaphone on my desk.

Betty: A dictaphone! I'll tell you about my dad sleeping in the ditches on the way here.

They exit.

Scene 12: Ghosts

Four Ghosts creep on stage and appear in frames.

MUSIC: SCARY GHOST MUSIC

Lady A: *(With her head through frame:)* Is that it? Is that all we get? A month-long exhibition to tell our stories? It won't do ...

Others: *(Sticking heads through frames and looking at **Lady A**:)* You're telling me it won't do!

All four talk at once ending with:

Suffragette: Whose history is it anyway? Come on!

Lady A: I have my honour to defend. Knickerbockers and seedy parties indeed. Classical music in the gallery -

MUSIC: TREMOLANDO G MAJOR - LIVE STRING QUARTET

Lady A: - and a very select crowd. Musicians from Corby still come and entertain the tenant farmers even now. A very genteel lot. *(Finding diary:)* See, the Vicar's wife always kept an accurate diary!

MUSIC: NETHERFIELD WALTZ - LIVE STRING QUARTET

Mrs Clarke:	*(Pre-recorded voice. Posh accent:)* "The Countess in full Countess Dress received her guests - (**Others** *stand up and become the guests as she hands them each a fan:)* - accompanied by the charming Lady Adela Cochraine in the spacious Hall where the smart Hungarian orchestra made music in the Minstrels' Gallery until the early hours of the morning."
Lady A:	Let the dancing begin!

MUSIC: POLKA DANCE MUSIC - LIVE STRING QUARTET

All four **Ghosts** *prepare to dance as the musicians start up a polka.* **Suffragette** *and* **Schoolmarm** *gallop around.*

Lady A:	Whoa! *(The music stops.)* Can we have something a little more stately please? I am a somewhat antiquated ghost!

MUSIC: BLUE DANUBE - LIVE STRING QUARTET

The **Ghosts** *dance, then sit down exhausted.*

Lady A:	Beautiful music. Now where was I? Ah yes. Knickerbockers. I wore my late first husband's uniform. It was eminently suited for riding a bicycle. Of course, there was considerably less of me in those days. Possibly all that exercise. And all those "so-called" affairs - people

were just jealous! I was appropriately chaperoned at all times, as was the custom of the day. In any case, what's a woman to do when her Spanish, spendthrift, good-for-nothing husband refuses to divorce her? And as for haunting the place ... well, if that's what they want, I can do a mean poltergeist! Where is that awful picture?

(She looks for things to destroy and kicks the bucket.)

Suffragette: Is that all you've got to complain about? That woman today was the first to show any interest in a long while. And what with the low turnout at the elections and the referendum on changing the voting system, there is still plenty to do! People seem to have forgotten what us Suffragettes went through to get women the vote in the first place. *(To women in the audience:)* And did you use yours? Some of us even died. Not just Emily Wilding Davidson either. Her death just appealed to the paparazzi. "Woman throws herself under the king's horse." My death was never reported. I wasn't famous, or middle-class. I died in Holloway jail. I'd been arrested for digging up a golf course. We only ever damaged property, not people. I went on hunger strike and was force-fed. They used to push a tube down your throat and pour food in through a funnel. At the point of starvation, they'd release you from prison until you recovered. But then they'd re-arrest you and it would start all over again. The Cat and Mouse Act, they called it. I was one of the ones who never recovered. At least you all died from natural causes.

Schoolmarm: Natural causes! I caught diphtheria from one of the kids. Bunch of diseased little beggars.

Farm Woman: *(To **Lady A**:)*
Rumour was, you got syphilis!

Lady A: I died of old age at 91, I'll have you know.

Suffragette: Anyway, this is my story. Looking on the positive side! The next exhibition is all about the Suffragettes. *(She finds the 'Votes for Women' sashes and hands them out to the other three, who get up and become Suffragettes.)* And at least they're learning that "Nana was a Suffragette" song, which actually says what we did. *(Self-importantly:)* Written for the opening of the Pankhurst Centre in Manchester, you know! Personally, I'd have preferred Ethyl Smythe's "March of the Women".

MUSIC: MARCH OF THE WOMEN - LIVE STRING QUARTET

All: (*Singing along:*) "March, march, many as one. Shoulder to shoulder and friend to friend!"

They all stand to attention.

Suffragette: We were all there. Just like old times. (*They freeze-frame, depicting women in a cell:*) Squashed up together in a cell. Scarcely room to breathe. (*She gets up and goes to the diary:*) I'd say your vicar's wife was not always so accurate - she writes nowhere of force-feeding, police brutality, torturing innocent women ...

*The other three **Women** take off their sashes, roll up their sleeves and turn into prison warders, then physicalise force-feeding **Suffragette.***

Mrs Clarke: (*Pre-recorded voice. Posh accent:*) "We felt we were living in ominous times. There were Home Rule disturbances in Ireland and at home. The *Times* newspaper gave a long list of assaults and outrages by Suffragettes who are causing great unrest and disturbance in London and elsewhere. Churches and other buildings were completely destroyed by fire. There came reports of disasters all over the world. In June the heir to the throne of Austria and his wife were assassinated. Austria then presented a demand to Serbia, and eventually war was declared."

F.W/S.M & L.A: *(Pushing **Suffragette** out of the chair)*
What did you do during the war?

Farm Worker: *(Confronting **Suffragette**:)* Gave up fighting for the vote and went off to join the war effort, making bullets and bombs and getting twice as much pay as us Irish women! Oh, there were some mighty fine battles right there on the shop floor, I can tell you!

MUSIC: IRISH JIG

Farm Worker *dances an Irish jig as she goes over to sit down in cottage.*

Farm Worker: I was very happy with how my story was told today - talking about the olden ways - hay ovens! And childcare whilst you lot were out fighting for the vote.

Schoolmarm: Childcare! I was looking after everyone's kids. Unless it was the harvest, and then you were quite happy to keep them off school.

Farm woman: A woman's place is in the home - keeping the hearth alight. No time for all this new-fangled nonsense.

Suffragette: You were happy to fight for equal pay to make bullets; it's all the same battle. We still haven't got Equal Pay. Thirty years on from Dagenham.

All:	Dagenham!
Suffragette:	Didn't you see that film "Made in Dagenham"? ... I saw it when I was haunting the Kettering Odeon.
Lady A:	I went to "Harry Potter".
Schoolmarm:	*(Looking around the schoolroom:)* Look at this excuse for a schoolroom. No child in my day would have dared to speak like that pushy young madam today. Seen and not heard. Unless they were singing, of course. At least she mentioned the music ... but she didn't talk about all the music festivals we won. Corby school was great for music. Always been a musical town.

*We hear singing coming closer. Enter **Choir** singing "Supercalifragilisticexpialidocious". The **Ghosts** hide behind their frames.*

Schoolmarm:	Seems the tradition is carrying on.

Anna comes on behind, looking through the syllabus.

Anna:	Super cali what? This word? It is impossible. And you tell me Polish is bad. I am able to choose a piece for the festival, so let's sing "The Inchworm".

***Betty** enters. Children see **Betty** and indicate to **Anna,** who turns.*

Betty: Don't let me interrupt! I'd love to listen to you.

Anna: OK.

Choir sings "The Inchworm". Then they march off boisterously singing "Supercalifragilisticexpialidocious". **Anna** *is still bowing and runs off after them.*

Scene 13: Diary

Betty: I wonder what it was really like. Will we ever know? I suppose we all need to use our imagination. This diary is handy. No-one would be interested in mine. Not even Rupert Murdoch! Monday: Cleaned the toilet. Tuesday: Went to the bingo. Wednesday: Took my mum for her radiotherapy. Nothing like Lady La-di-dah.

Betty is at the drawing room table reading the diary.

MUSIC: BAROQUE MUSIC - LIVE RECORDER CONSORT

Mrs Clarke: *(Pre-recorded voice. Posh accent:)* After a time in commemoration of the peace, we gave for the Corby choir and choral society a musical entertainment. Professor Dolmetsch, with his son and daughter, illustrated his very interesting lecture on early English music with Elizabethan instruments and delightful dances by his little daughter in accompanying Shakespearean songs.

Betty: It's amazing how often music is mentioned in these books and diaries. I reckon there was a wider range of music then than now. I mean some groups are still in existence. Corby Choral Society and the Silver Band are both over 100 years old. You just don't hear so much about them now. The band gets mentioned in the account of the protest when they tried to shut down the brickworks all those years ago. Most people think the Silver Band Club is just a place to drink - my man drinks up there. Listens to them play sometimes. Says they're really good. Anyway, may as well have music while I work.

*She puts on a record and we hear brass instruments. The **Band** appears amongst the audience.*

Betty: What was in that tea? This place gives me the creeps after dark. I'm off.

***Betty** exits.*

Scene 14: Memorial 2

Band come on and stand around the memorial and play a tune. Cast re-enter and gather round war memorial. Band plays "I vow to thee my country", then 11 o'clock chimes.

WMW: With each white poppy for peace, we recall a life lost or ruined through war. Nearly 100 years after the war to end all wars, with 10 million children alone killed in the last decade.

All: We choose to remember all the victims of war.

Group 1:   Men.

Group 2:   Women.

Group 3:   And children.

We have a repeat of the opening ceremony, but this time with up-to-date names of current conflicts and white poppies. The following list is not complete and since the play was written there have been many more wars. It is important to allow the cast to choose. At the time of printing, the illegal invasion of Ukraine by Russia, is exactly one year old.

Each woman steps forward as she says the name of a war or conflict and throws a white poppy onto the stage.

Women in turn: Chile, Guatemala, Mau Mau uprising in Kenya, Spanish Civil War, Oswiecim – Auschwitz, Polish/Ukrainian war, Northern Ireland, Iran/Iraq war,

Rwanda, Uganda, Gulf War, Black September, Iraq, World War II, Vietnam, Cuban revolution, Afghanistan, Battle of Culloden, Libya, Arab/Israeli war, Apartheid in South Africa, the Intifada, the Korean War

*All turn to the **Bugler**.*

MUSIC: THE LAST POST

All:　　　　(*Turning to face the audience on cue:*)
　　　　　　　We remember, lest we forget.

CURTAIN

About the author

As a playwright and theatre director, Paula has written and staged over fifty plays for Corby Women's Theatre Group and Shout! Youth Theatre. Her play *Women of Steel* which tells the story of Corby through the eyes of women and children became a book which received critical acclaim as an accurate and accessible living history of a proud former Steel town and its people.

In 2016 Paula composed the *Sounds of Home Suite*, an orchestral work based on interviews with people from over thirty countries who had chosen Corby as their home. In 2019 she was commissioned to write her debut composition for brass bands, *Impressions of Barnwell*.

During the COVID lockdown in 2020 she published two books about Kingswood, her local nature reserve where she teaches Forest School.

Impressions of an English Woodland was her first book of poetry and *Inspiring Kingswood* her first children's book.

Archiving the 20-year history of Shout! during 2020-2022, resulted in a film, a website, the Steel Kids book, and playscripts for schools.

Paula continues to create documentary theatre about her town – most recently in 2023 – *"The Planks Gave Way"* for the GMB Union's 25th commemoration of Worker's Memorial Day.

She is also a committed lifelong campaigner for women's rights, having co-founded and volunteered at the town's Women's Centre for over 20 years. She is currently engaged in lesbian rights activism.

A talented musician, hill-walker and nature-lover, she is a great believer in getting things done.

Acknowledgements

The creation of this book was made possible by a grant from Northamptonshire Community Foundation and an anonymous donor – you know who you are!

Thanks to the tireless team at Lunarlink Publishing: Val Stein for proofreading and Antonia Burrows for editing.

Thanks also to Kate Anderson for your creative design and Craig for your typesetting.

This book had input from too many people to list here but, as ever, all of you who discussed the concept, helped shape the content, and read the early versions - have my heartfelt appreciation. Your honest feedback and reality checks were a vital part of the process.

And to all who ever took part in one of Corby Women's Theatre group productions or bared your soul to share the true stories upon which these plays are based – thankyou.

Together we have created a record of women's lives past and present. A vital piece of herstory.

Paula Boulton

Milton Keynes UK
Ingram Content Group UK Ltd.
UKHW021046111023
430366UK00001B/2

9 781906 482091